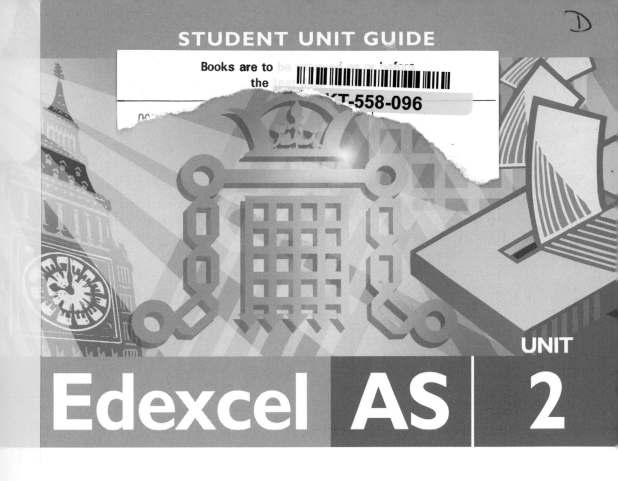

UNIT

Edexcel AS | 2

Government & Politics

Governing the UK

Chris Robinson

Philip Allan Updates, an imprint of Hodder Education, part of Hachette UK, Market Place, Deddington, Oxfordshire OX15 OSE

Orders
Bookpoint Ltd, 130 Milton Park, Abingdon, Oxfordshire OX14 4SB
tel: 01235 827720
fax: 01235 400454
e-mail: uk.orders@bookpoint.co.uk
Lines are open 9.00 a.m.–5.00 p.m., Monday to Saturday, with a 24-hour message answering service. You can also order through the Philip Allan Updates website: www.philipallan.co.uk

ISBN 978-0-340-94974-0

First printed 2008
Impression number 5 4 3 2
Year 2013 2012 2011 2010 2009 2008

This guide has been written specifically to support students preparing for the Edexcel AS Government & Politics Unit 2 examination. The content has been neither approved nor endorsed by Edexcel and remains the sole responsibility of the author.

Typeset by Phoenix Photosetting, Chatham, Kent
Printed by MPG Books, Bodmin

Hachette UK's policy is to use papers that are natural, renewable and recyclable products and made from wood grown in sustainable forests. The logging and manufacturing processes are expected to conform to the environmental regulations of the country of origin.

Contents

Introduction

■ ■ ■

Content Guidance

Constitutions

Parliament

The executive

The judiciary and civil liberties

■ ■ ■

Questions and Answers

Introduction

The aim of this guide is to prepare students for the Unit 2 Governing the UK examination for the Edexcel Advanced Subsidiary (AS) GCE in Government & Politics. Unit 2 deals with some of the major governmental processes and key institutions in UK politics. Some topics in this unit develop themes learned earlier in the AS course, while others may be seen as essential building blocks for the remainder of the course. The specification for Governing the UK is divided into four main topics:

(1) **The constitution:** the nature of the constitution; different types of constitution; the main sources and features of the UK constitution; sovereignty and the constitution; reforming the constitution.

(2) **Parliament:** the role and powers of Parliament and how effective Parliament is in carrying them out, with particular emphasis on the relationship between Parliament and the executive; reforming Parliament.

(3) **The prime minister and the cabinet:** their roles; the core executive; powers/constraints and sources of the powers of the prime minister; prime ministerial leadership; changing relationships with other political players (e.g. parties, cabinet, Parliament); presidential politics.

(4) **The judiciary and civil liberties:** the rule of law; issues of judicial independence and judicial neutrality; civil liberties and individual rights.

How to use this guide

- This **Introduction** contains information about both the scheme of assessment and the format of the unit test. In addition, there is advice on the different strategies required for dealing with the varying types of questions on the examination paper.
- The **Content Guidance** section summarises the knowledge and skills needed to succeed in the Unit 2 examination. It provides an overview of each topic and focuses on the themes that most commonly arise in the examination. The key skills that are essential for developing arguments in particular topics are also covered.
- The **Questions and Answers** section contains a range of questions which might be found on the Governing the UK exam paper. The answers and examiner comments focus on the essentials needed to gain high marks.

Scheme of assessment

The AS GCE has a weighting of 50% when carried forward towards the full A-level GCE. The structure of the AS course is as follows:

Unit	Assessment method	Length	Objectives assessed
1	Written — 2 structured questions from a choice of 4	1 hour 20 minutes	1 (50%), 2 (30%), 3 (20%)
2	Written — 1 stimulus-based question from a choice of 2 and 1 essay question from a choice of 2	1 hour 20 minutes	1 (50%), 2 (30%), 3 (20%)

There are three assessment objectives (AOs), or sets of skills, that you will be tested on in the examination. In Unit 2, AO1 has a higher weighting than AO2 or AO3. The skills required by each AO are shown in the table below.

Assessment objective	Skills required	Unit 2 weighting
AO1	demonstrate knowledge and understanding of relevant institutions, processes, political concepts, theories and debates	50%
AO2	analyse and evaluate political information, arguments and explanations, and identify parallels, connections, similarities and differences between the aspects of the political systems studied	30%
AO3	construct and communicate coherent arguments making use of a range of appropriate political vocabulary	20%

Exam format

Unit 2 is assessed in a 1-hour-20-minute exam. In this time you have to answer two questions — one stimulus-based question out of a choice of two and one extended question from a choice of two. Both questions are worth a total of 40 marks each. You should divide your time equally, with 40 minutes to answer each question. Since there are 40 minutes available in which to gain 40 marks, you should allocate 1 mark to each minute.

Note that the stimulus-based questions are subdivided into three parts.

- **Part (a): 5 marks (5 minutes approximately)**
  This question requires a short, concise answer, based on the source material. The source could take the form of a passage of text or a table, or both. A couple of relevant points, briefly explained, with an example if appropriate, is all that is needed to gain full marks. One useful practice technique is to find out how much you can write in 5 minutes. This can act as a rough guide to how long your answer should be.

- **Part (b): 10 marks (10 minutes approximately)**

  Clearly, more substance is expected in answers to part (b) questions than part (a) ones. The question is worded so as to enable answers to draw on information in the source material and on your own knowledge. You should make a number of points, supported by explanations and evidence in the form of appropriate examples, quotations or data. Of the 10 marks allocated to this question, 3 are AO2 marks, which means candidates will be expected to offer some evaluation if they hope to achieve a very high mark.

- **Part (c): 25 marks (25 minutes approximately)**

  In this part of the question, you are expected to move away from the source material and to base much of your answer on your own knowledge. A longer response is required, based on an issue relating to the topic in the source material and with examples given. To achieve the higher range of marks, you are expected to explain a number of points in support of a particular argument. Only 8 of the 25 marks on offer are for the AO1 skills of knowledge, understanding and recall. There are 9 marks for AO2 (analysis and evaluation). Finally, 8 of the marks are awarded for the quality of written communication (AO3). Candidates will notice an asterisk (*) beside each part (c) question on the exam paper. This draws attention to the importance of the quality of written communication in this examination. A candidate who merely offers a list of facts is likely to achieve only 6 or 7 marks, given that 17 of the 25 on offer are for evaluation, analysis and written communication. If a question begins 'To what extent...' or 'What are the advantages and disadvantages of...', you must give both sides of the argument in order to achieve high marks.

- **The extended question: 40 marks (40 minutes approximately)**

  AS Government & Politics now requires more practice in the skills of essay writing, as candidates must answer one of the two extended questions. These are designed to assess how well you can construct a substantial series of arguments around a particular debate, without the aid of subsection questions to act as a guide. There is no set length for these questions, but with 40 minutes in which to complete the essay, it is unlikely that you will access marks from across the range available without explaining and illustrating a number of points well. Again, it may be useful to find out how many words you are physically capable of writing in the set time period. Remember, if you are used to word-processing your written assignments for your teachers, it is likely that you will get writer's hand fatigue when you start writing extended pieces of work by hand. You should practise this in advance of the exam.

Examination skills

Read the questions

At the beginning of the examination, take time to read the question paper properly. If you have revised well for a topic, there is a temptation to react with excitement if you see the relevant words in the question and to ignore almost entirely the context in which the question is being asked.

When reading a question, look for the key words on which your answer will hinge. The words indicating the topic are rarely the key words in a question. Consider the following example:

(c) Should the UK's constitution remain uncodified?   **(40 marks)**

The question is requesting points on *both* sides of the debate about whether a codified constitution is a good thing or not. Clearly, if you only provide arguments in favour of or against codified constitutions, you will not be able to access the whole range of marks on offer. Conversely, if you write everything there is to know about codified constitutions you may not gain any extra marks and will have wasted valuable time. This might appear obvious, but you would be surprised how many candidates missed the key words when this question was set. Practise finding the key words in questions on old exam papers.

Plan your answers

Some candidates write plans for all their answers at the beginning of the exam. Although this takes time, it can be beneficial and plans do not have to be exhaustive — simple bullet points are normally sufficient. If you plan your answer to all parts of a question before you start writing, you can be sure that you will have enough information to answer part (c) effectively. It is far better to spend a few minutes doing this than to get to part (c) of a question and realise that you do not know enough to answer it.

Plans help you to order and reorder your ideas before committing them to paper. They enable you to build up your essay in a logical way that is more likely to impress an examiner than randomly stated points. Plans can also come in useful if you run out of time. If your plan remains on script, without crossings out, the examiner will consider the points made in it and give you some credit for them, especially if you annotate them.

Follow the rubric

Following the rules (or rubric) of the examination is vital. This unit test contains specific instructions. There are two types of question to answer (stimulus-based and extended). The stimulus-based question is divided into three parts, with different marks for each. You must answer the correct number of questions. If you fail to answer one, your overall mark will be seriously reduced as a result. Similarly, if you answer more than two questions, your overall mark will be reduced because there is not enough time to answer more than two questions properly.

The extended question is a new development for the Edexcel AS in Government & Politics and requires an essay-length response. Given that you have 40 minutes to answer this question, a single side of writing is unlikely to achieve very good marks. Consider how much work is required for part (c) of the stimulus-based question, for which you should allocate 25 minutes.

You should be familiar with the format of the exam. Copies of past papers can be obtained from Edexcel after the first examinations in June 2009. Specimen papers and the subject specification are available on the Edexcel website at **www.edexcel.org.uk**.

Manage your time

Organising your time in the examination is just as crucial as good preparation before-hand. All examination rooms must have clearly visible clocks and you should jot down somewhere, either on the question paper or answer book, the times by which you should be beginning each new question. You should then keep to this timetable.

Although it is tempting to devote disproportionate time to questions you know you can answer well, it is not advisable to spend too long on the 5-mark questions — no matter how much you write, the maximum you can achieve is 5 marks. A 5-mark question will require less time than a 10-mark question, which in turn will require less than half the time of a 25-mark question.

The best way to learn how to manage time is to practise. Use the Questions and Answers section in this book to practise your examination technique against the clock.

Practical tips

- **Do questions have to be answered in any particular order?** No. Some candidates offer what they consider to be their strongest answer first. This approach can help to focus your mind and boost your confidence.
- **Some candidates deliberately leave their responses to the very short answer questions until the end of the paper. Is this advisable?** There is some logic to this practice, particularly if you are worried about time management. However, badly answered questions, whether short or long, will lose marks.
- **What should you do if there are only 10 minutes left and you still have a part (c) to answer?** With only 10 minutes left, the best thing to do is to convert a plan into a series of briefly explained bullet points. Although this will not earn as many marks as a full answer, it is likely to achieve a better mark than a partial response that ends 'Sorry, ran out of time'. It is important to remember that time management is a skill which is implicitly being assessed in the examination, and that weakness in this respect will cost marks.
- **What should you do if you are not short of time, but feel there are no more questions you can answer?** One thing is certain in examinations: if you do not attempt a question you will earn no marks for it. It is better to answer a question badly than not to attempt it at all. Even if you only earn 7 or 8 marks out of 25 for a part (c) answer, this could make the difference between a grade E and a grade C.

Content
Guidance

This section outlines the key content of the AS specification for Unit 2. It is broken down into the four main topics assessed in the Unit 2 test:

(1) Constitutions
This topic discusses the nature of the constitution, different types of constitution and constitutional arrangements, giving an insight into how and where these work. It also considers the advantages and disadvantages of codified and uncodified constitutions, and the issue of constitutional reform.

(2) Parliament
The composition, role, functions and effectiveness of the UK Parliament are examined in this topic. It also covers the differences between parliamentary government and presidential government, as well as the relationship of Parliament to the European Union and the devolved assemblies. Parliamentary reform is examined too.

(3) The prime minister and cabinet
This topic examines power within the UK core executive, the role of the prime minister and the cabinet. It considers political leadership, the power of the prime minister, relations with political parties and factors constraining the prime minister's power. The debate about the presidentialisation of UK politics is also covered.

(4) Judges and civil liberties
The rights and freedoms enjoyed by UK citizens are the focus here. The topic examines the rule of law and the roles of the judiciary, the extent to which judges are independent of other political institutions, the ability of judges to check the role of the executive and whether judges can carry out their function in a neutral and unbiased manner. Issues arising out of the passing of the Human Rights Act and the relationships between the judiciary, the European courts and EU law are also considered.

Constitutions

What is a constitution?

In the context of political science, a constitution is a set of rules that establishes the powers of political institutions, and the limits that may be placed on those powers — for example, the powers of the executive or the authority of the courts. A constitution may also indicate the relationship between the state and the citizen by outlining the rights that citizens may expect to enjoy. Constitutionalism refers to the situation where government is regulated by a constitution, normally codified (see below).

Recently there has been much debate about the European Union constitution (see below), with some critics arguing that only countries have constitutions. But in fact it is not just states that have constitutions; societies, clubs and charitable organisations also have them, often in the form of rule books.

Common elements of a constitution

Below are some of the elements that may be defined within a constitution:
- the length of time between elections
- eligibility to vote
- the rights and duties of the citizen
- the extent and the limits of government power
- the powers of the judiciary
- the manner in which governments are formed
- the role and powers of the legislature
- the role and powers of the head of state
- the relationship between central government and government at a sub-national level

This is not an exhaustive list, but a descriptive guide as to what one might expect to find in a constitution.

Core institutions

Constitutions may vary from one country to another, but all constitutions have to enable the passing of laws, and the execution and upholding of those laws. It is common, therefore, for the following core institutions to be present in constitutions, regardless of the type.

Legislature

'Legislature' is another name for a parliament or national assembly, and it is so called because it is where legislation (law) is discussed and made. In the UK, the House of

Commons and the House of Lords (and technically the monarch) make up Parliament. In the United States, the legislature is called Congress and is made up of the Senate and the House of Representatives.

Executive

This is the name given to the government, which is responsible for the day-to-day running of the state through the execution and administration of policies and laws. In the UK, government ministers are the executive and the prime minister is head of government, with the civil service acting as the administrative arm of the executive. In the United States, the president is the head of the executive (or head of government). The US president is also the head of state, whereas in the UK this position is held by the monarch.

Judiciary

The judiciary is the name given to the institution responsible for the interpretation and enforcement of the laws through the courts. It is for the judges to ensure that the rule of law is upheld and that those who break the law are dealt with appropriately. This includes politicians and ministers, none of whom are above the law. Indeed, any judge who considers that a minister has exceeded his or her powers (those allowed by statute) may declare the action *ultra vires* — literally, beyond the powers — and a change in the law would be required to make the action legal. In the United States, Supreme Court judges may rule an action unconstitutional, and in these circumstances an amendment or change to the Constitution is required. This is difficult to achieve (see below).

Fusion and separation of powers

Fusion of powers

In the United Kingdom, the legislative, executive and judicial functions overlap. This is known as the fusion of powers. Figure 1 shows a diagrammatic representation of this fusion.

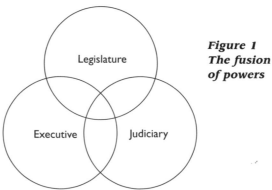

Figure 1
The fusion
of powers

The overlap between the legislative and executive functions relates to those individuals who are both Members of Parliament and members of the executive, in other words government ministers.

Another overlap occurs between the legislature and the judiciary. This relates to the Law Lords, the senior judges who sit in the House of Lords.

Separation of powers

In other constitutions, the main powers of state may be kept separate from one another, with no overlaps of the type that may be seen in the UK constitution. The US Constitution was designed in this manner in order to prevent over-concentration of power in the hands of one person or one political institution.

Figure 2 gives a diagrammatic representation of the separation of powers. The executive and the legislature do not overlap; in other words, members of the government are not also members of the legislature. In the United States, for example, the president is elected separately and does not draw cabinet members from either house of Congress.

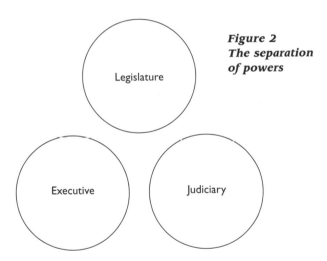

Figure 2
The separation
of powers

In a country that has a separation of powers, the judiciary is more independent from the other political institutions of the state. In the United States, the president may appoint judges to the Supreme Court, but cannot dismiss them. This is said to add further checks and balances to the political system.

Types of constitutions

Codified and uncodified constitutions

Codified constitutions

> **Tip**
>
> You may find references to so-called 'written' constitutions in some older textbooks.
> In the examination, however, reference will only be made to the term 'codified'.

A codified constitution is one where all the rules relating to the powers of the political institutions of the state and the rights of citizens are located together in a single, written document. In fact, most countries in the world have a constitution that is codified. Examples include Germany, whose constitution was drawn up by the occupying powers after the Second World War, and France, where the current constitution dates to the late 1950s. But perhaps the most famous example of a country with a codified constitution is the United States; this dates back to the late eighteenth century.

In the US Constitution there are articles relating to the president, the Supreme Court, the House of Representatives and the Senate (Congress), as well as the individual states. Additionally, there are amendments (changes) to the Constitution. The first ten of these (collectively known as the Bill of Rights) specify some of the key rights that US citizens enjoy.

In order to amend a codified constitution, it is usually necessary to achieve a high level of agreement about the changes that are proposed. The US Constitution can only be changed with the agreement of two-thirds of both houses of Congress and three-quarters of all the state legislatures. This is a very difficult level of consensus to achieve, and consequently there have been only 27 amendments to the US Constitution in more than 200 years.

Codified constitutions may be adopted by intergovernmental organisations as well as individual nation-states. There have been a number of attempts to form all the treaties of the European Union into a codified constitution. These ran into difficulties in 2005. In December 2007, EU members signed the Lisbon Treaty, which many believe is a codified constitution in all but name.

Uncodified constitutions

There are not many examples of uncodified constitutions, but the United Kingdom is one. Rather than having rules relating to the powers of the political institutions of state and the rights of citizens set out together in a single document, the UK constitution is drawn from a number of different sources, both written and unwritten, as follows:

- **Statute.** This is another word for law that has been passed by Parliament. All legislation must have the approval of Parliament; crucially, this includes laws that regulate the constitution itself. The 1969 Representation of the People Act lowered the voting age in UK elections from 21 to 18. This Act was passed in the same way as other laws. In the United States, the reduction of the voting age from 21 to 18 required an amendment to the Constitution (the 26th Amendment, ratified in 1971).

- **Conventions.** These are the customary and accepted practices that have evolved over many years, so that they represent something fixed by tradition. In the UK, the constitution has many such conventions, including the holding of general elections on a Thursday, or that ministers should take responsibility for any mistakes made in their departments and resign. There is no law to enforce these conventions, and they rely entirely on the consent and goodwill of all engaged in the political process.

- **Common law.** This is law made by judges in their rulings on specific cases. These rulings have traditionally been used to help other judges with their deliberations on similar cases. Unlike statute, common law is not found as written legislation, although much is written about the principles of common law as it applies to notable past legal cases, and to contemporary issues where the same principles may apply. Much common law derives from decisions made many centuries ago.

- **Written works of constitutional importance.** There are a number of milestones in the ongoing commentary on the constitution in the UK. These interpretations are, on occasion, a definitive view of a particular political institution. Thomas Erskine May's *Treatise upon the Law, Privileges, Proceedings, and Usage of Parliament* and its updated editions is seen as the definitive guide to the rules of conduct for Members of Parliament. *The English Constitution* by Walter Bagehot, first published in 1867, is an account of the history and workings of the British political system. The book is regarded as key in its analysis of the monarchy, the role of the prime minister and cabinet, and comparisons with the American presidential system.

- **Treaties.** Perhaps the most important treaties are the numerous ones the United Kingdom has signed since joining what is now the European Union. The Treaty of Rome, which was signed on accession in 1972, effectively determines a number of policy areas such as trade and agriculture. The governments of EU member states have already agreed that these treaties should be merged into a European constitution. This would be a new source of the uncodified United Kingdom constitution. However, referendums in France and the Netherlands have cast much doubt on whether this constitution will ever come into being.

The number of amendments to the UK's uncodified constitution (many made between 1997 and 2005) demonstrates the relative ease with which such a constitution can be changed, especially in contrast with the number of amendments to the US Constitution over the past 200 years. It may be argued, however, that the reforms that took place in the period 1997–2005 are not typical. In the Conservative administrations of Margaret Thatcher (1979–90) and John Major (1990–97), there were relatively few changes to the constitution. So care should be taken in judging the uncodified constitution in the UK on the basis of just a few recent years of history.

Unitary and federal constitutions

Unitary constitutions

The United Kingdom is said to have a unitary constitution. The term relates to the way in which power in the state derives from one single source or place. In the UK, because Parliament is sovereign, all the powers of other political institutions at national and sub-national level derive from the authority of Parliament. This means that any political institution in the UK can be abolished if Parliament wishes it.

The implication of a unitary constitution is that it is likely to be centralised, with much power residing with the party that controls Parliament. Local and devolved governments have no intrinsic rights to exist, except as Parliament wills. In 1986 the Greater London Council and several other metropolitan authorities in the conurbations of the West Midlands, Greater Manchester, West Yorkshire and elsewhere were abolished by the Thatcher government. Similarly, a future government could use its parliamentary majority to abolish the devolved assemblies in Scotland and Wales. The fact that the UK does not have a codified constitution, combined with its unitary nature, means that considerable power is vested in a strong government.

Some countries that have codified constitutions also have a unitary constitution. France, for example, has a highly centralised political culture but all the political institutions of state are currently regulated by the constitution of the Fifth Republic.

Federal constitutions

The federal type of constitution is based on the principle that political power is not concentrated in one central place. In the United States, this ties in with the separation of powers (see page 13). A federal constitutional structure ensures that power and authority are also held in regions of a country. In the US, there are 50 states, and each has its own legislature and the ability to determine much of the law within its own jurisdiction. Any visitor to the US is struck by the variation that exists between states on matters ranging from speed limits and taxation to education and law enforcement.

An example of a federal state closer to home is Germany. Federal structures often assume that powers reside at the local level except where the constitution declares otherwise. In this sense, there are different assumptions in such countries about what powers central government should enjoy.

The federal structure would normally be maintained by a codified constitution.

The debate about codified and uncodified constitutions

Tip

In the AS examination, the questions may focus on either codified or uncodified constitutions, or on the advantages and/or disadvantages of each.

Some politicians in the UK, especially Liberal Democrats, have argued that the country should adopt a codified constitution along the lines of those in the United States and member states of the European Union.

Features of the UK constitution

By now some of the key features of the UK constitution should be apparent. First, the constitution is uncodified; it is instead derived from a number of sources, both written and unwritten. Second, the UK constitution may be said to be flexible because it is relatively easy to amend to meet changing circumstances. Finally, the UK constitution is unitary, in that all power derives from a single, central authority.

The case for an uncodified constitution

The first point to be made about an uncodified constitution is its flexibility. In the UK, the constitution is easy to change compared to the convoluted process that is required to amend the Constitution in the United States, for example; in the UK, an Act of Parliament is technically all that is needed to secure a change in the constitution. The benefit of this is that it enables the political system to adapt quickly to changing circumstances and to provide an adequate response to new situations. In the aftermath of the terrorist attacks in the United States on 11 September 2001, the UK government was able to change with relative ease the scope of the Human Rights Act in respect of terrorist offences. In this respect it may be argued that an uncodified constitution can be better kept up to date.

It may also be argued that an uncodified constitution provides strong government in the UK. Governments are able to carry out their legislative programme without undue interference from other institutions in the political system, as long as these actions remain within the law. This means that citizens can expect to see the government implement its manifesto pledges between general elections. This may be contrasted with the United States, where the president and Congress may find themselves in conflict over issues, leading to inaction. In the mid-1990s, President Clinton, the Democratic president of the US, was at loggerheads with the House of Representatives, in which the Republicans held a majority. Their inability to agree over federal budget issues left Washington, DC in gridlock for some weeks.

Further to the above point, there is clear accountability for the UK government. Since it is able to carry out its programme, the people can apportion credit or blame accordingly. A government may try, but it usually cannot succeed, to blame other institutions for its own omissions or mistakes. A codified constitution is more likely to bring a blurring of accountability, and again the United States provides an insight into this; in the above-mentioned stalemate between President Clinton and the House of Representatives in 1995, it was difficult for many people to apportion blame accurately. Although President Clinton appeared to win in terms of popular opinion, many on the Republican side believed that an injustice was done.

Despite lacking the institutional anchors that hold down and stabilise a codified constitution, it may be argued that an uncodified constitution also establishes conventions and traditions which are hard to change. Admittedly, any government determined to get its own way can use its majority in the House of Commons to force changes, but the controversy that can rage as a consequence of a government wishing to alter the way in which conventions operate can prove to be a deterrent and a brake on reforming administrations. As a result, although there have been changes to certain parliamentary procedures, such as the timing and frequency of Prime Minister's Question Time, many of the procedures of Parliament continue untouched, as they have done for over a century. Where major changes have taken place, they have been in response to calls for reform and have, on the whole, been welcomed, with only some dissent. Most MPs would not question the value of the departmental select committee system, which was introduced shortly after the election of Margaret Thatcher as prime minister in 1979.

The case for a codified constitution

A codified constitution gives a clear statement of the distribution of political power within a country. On the issue of accountability, a codified constitution helps citizens identify those persons and institutions responsible for particular actions. In the United States and France, the people elect their presidents separately from their national assemblies. It may be argued that ordinary parliamentary representatives do not share the blame for mistakes that may be made by political leaders. There is some evidence in the United States that voters do make sophisticated distinctions about who or what they are voting for in the various elections, and that they 'split the ticket' — in other words, they support different parties in different elections. For example, they may vote for a Democratic presidential candidate while voting for a Republican congressional candidate.

One of the main reasons given for supporting a codified constitution is that it can limit the power of the executive. Lord Hailsham famously spoke of the 'elective dictatorship' — the idea that a UK government with a parliamentary majority can do just about what it wants. There are few restrictions on government in the UK and it could be argued that a constitution that determined the limits of executive powers would be more democratic. It may also be argued that having some form of US-style statute of limitations, to restrict the term of office of a prime minister, might lead to better and more responsive politics.

A codified constitution that was difficult to amend would protect citizens from governments changing fundamental laws for the sake of political expediency. The changes to the Human Rights Act after 11 September 2001 might be regarded as initiated by a government more interested in control than in countering terrorism.

However, a codified constitution does not prevent controversial alterations being made. The 18th Amendment to the US Constitution outlawed the production, sale and consumption of alcohol for beverage purposes in the 1920s. This was the product of some very timely and effective lobbying and publicity by temperance groups. America suddenly found alcohol banned, and one direct consequence was the rise of organised crime in the 1920s in some of the largest US cities. One instance can hardly be used to demolish the case for a codified constitution, however; indeed the scarcity of such examples may make this the exception that proves the rule.

The final point to make in this debate is about the rights of citizens. Many codified constitutions contain an entrenched set of rights which cannot be tampered with without widespread political and popular support. In the United States, the Bill of Rights is effectively the first ten amendments to the Constitution. These rights cannot be changed easily, and citizens are taught exactly what their fundamental rights are. By contrast, rights in the United Kingdom may be altered relatively easily. This, it may be argued, does not provide the citizen with protection from a potentially unscrupulous government.

Sovereignty

Sovereignty refers to the ultimate power that may be exercised within a state. It may be determined by some form of constitutional settlement, or simply by historical convention. Sovereignty also sets apart the jurisdiction between different states. It may be classified in particular ways.

At this level of study, it is useful to distinguish between political sovereignty and legal sovereignty. In the United Kingdom, **political sovereignty** is said to be expressed by the people at the time of a general election. At this time it is the voters who exercise the ultimate decision-making power by electing a 'new' House of Commons, which in turn legitimises the party in government. Clearly, this type of sovereignty is periodic, coming around only once every 4 or 5 years.

Legal sovereignty lies in the body that effectively makes the key political decisions in the state. In the UK, Parliament is regarded as legally sovereign, since it is there that all decisions are endorsed.

The UK constitution in the EU context

The United Kingdom joined the European Economic Community (now the European Union) in 1973. There was a big debate about the issue, and this debate cut across party lines. Some figures of the left and right believed that the UK constitution would be damaged if it joined the EEC. In particular there was a worry that membership would reduce the sovereignty of the UK. The concern was that the UK Parliament could effectively be overruled in a series of decisions taken by unelected and non-accountable officials in Brussels.

The national parliaments of member states cannot overrule EU law. The *Factortame* case illustrates this point — the European Court of Justice struck down UK fisheries legislation that ran contrary to EU law.

However, European Union law is presently confined to a limited number of areas. Key policy areas, such as the economy, law and order, welfare, education and foreign affairs, are not covered by EU law and it is unlikely that any government, regardless of its political persuasion, would want to give up control of these matters.

Ultimately, of course, the United Kingdom can leave the EU if it wishes. Members of the United Kingdom Independence Party believe this is what should happen, because the threat of the EU to UK sovereignty is too great. The main political parties, however, believe that the benefits of membership of the EU outweigh the costs and that trying to reform the organisation from within is the best way to safeguard the interests of the United Kingdom.

It could be argued that sovereignty can be measured by the capacity of the UK to withdraw from the EU by simply tearing up all the treaties that it has signed and repealing all the associated European legislation. Theoretically this may be true, but apart from some Eurosceptics in the Conservative Party and groups such as UKIP, many believe that it would be difficult for such a thing to happen without causing major economic difficulties to the UK. In this way, critics of the EU argue, real and effective sovereignty has been permanently eroded.

Sovereignty and devolution

After the 1997 general election the Blair government introduced devolution, first for Scotland and Wales and then for Northern Ireland. Devolution involves a large degree of self-government and directly elected national assemblies.

With devolution, sovereignty resides in a central authority, but certain powers are handed down to sub-national bodies. The Westminster Parliament retains the right to alter these powers (to remove some of them, for example) or to abolish the sub-national bodies entirely. Devolution does not entail any fixed amount of power transferred from the national to sub-national level. Indeed, if you look at devolution across the UK, a number of models may be observed, each with different amounts of power.

Although the unitary nature of the UK constitution means that, technically, devolved assemblies could be abolished by Westminster, it is difficult to see how this could happen realistically, for example in the face of public opinion in Scotland. It could be argued, therefore, that since 1997 effective sovereignty (as opposed to theoretical sovereignty) has shifted within the UK.

Constitutional reform

Labour's post-1997 reforms

Following the 1997 general election, in which Labour came to power, a number of reforms to the UK constitution were implemented. In fact, much of the emphasis of the first Blair government (1997–2001) was placed upon this area of policy. The reforms can be summarised as follows:

- devolution
- human rights legislation
- electoral reform

Devolution

Devolution was introduced in Scotland and Wales after successful referendums in 1997. Scotland voted for a parliament with tax-varying and primary legislative powers. Wales narrowly voted in favour of an assembly with administrative devolution. In addition, the UK government secured the consent of the people of Northern Ireland for a new devolved assembly in the province. The reforms in Northern Ireland are, arguably, the only way to achieve peace in the province, by providing a voice for minority opinion. From 2000, London had its first city-wide elected authority since the 1980s.

Human rights legislation

In 1998 the European Convention on Human Rights was incorporated into UK law in the form of the Human Rights Act. For the first time, rights such as freedom of speech and fair trial were written into law. Citizens no longer have to go to the European Court of Human Rights in Strasbourg in order to have their rights protected.

Electoral reform

Changes to the UK's electoral systems have come about either in their own right or in conjunction with other reforms that have taken place. For example, the devolved bodies in Edinburgh, Cardiff and Belfast are all elected using various proportional electoral systems.

Elections to the Greater London Authority are also conducted under a proportional system. The London mayor is elected every 4 years using the supplementary vote system. Since 1999, UK elections to the European Parliament have been run using a version of the party list system. Before that time, these elections used the simple plurality (first-past-the-post) system. (For more detail about alternative electoral systems in the UK, see Philip Allan Updates' *Edexcel AS Government & Politics* Unit 1 Guide: *People and Politics*.)

Elected mayors

Blair's government was keen to introduce US-style, directly elected mayors in some of the UK's major cities. Referendums have been held in towns such as Doncaster and Hartlepool, and, where there was a 'yes' vote, the newly elected mayors assumed a number of authority-wide strategic powers.

Electoral reform for general elections

A referendum on House of Commons electoral reform was promised by Blair's Labour government in 1997, but following the 1998 recommendations of the Jenkins Commission, nothing more was said on the matter. It may be claimed that the government perhaps saw no benefit for itself in reforming the voting system, since any changes would certainly have seen Labour losing its parliamentary majority.

The Labour Party remained divided, both on whether reform was desirable and on which system would be best to replace first-past-the-post. Indeed, any attempts to introduce reform were likely to provoke dissent from some quarters of the party.

The government also viewed such legislation as clogging up the parliamentary timetable and delaying what it believed to be more important matters. Furthermore, the government was concerned that the public might think it attached more importance to this area than other issues, such as health, education and crime.

English regional assemblies

Despite the enthusiasm of the Labour deputy prime minister, John Prescott, this aspect of devolution was put aside after a 2004 referendum in the northeast of England revealed low public support for regional assemblies.

Assessment: praise for Labour's reforms

Devolution

The Scots and the Welsh are now governed by devolved bodies that are closer to the people and therefore more responsive to their needs. In Scotland it is argued that, as a consequence of the coalition administrations, there is greater consensual politics, based on moderation and agreement. These changes have enabled the Scottish Parliament in particular to tailor policies to the particular interests of its people.

Human rights legislation

The Human Rights Act has set down for the first time the rights that UK citizens should expect and has brought the UK into line with other European countries. A key criticism of the status of rights in the UK before the introduction of the Act was that they were vulnerable to the whim of Parliament. It was also claimed that a feature of the UK constitution in the postwar era was the gradual erosion of citizens' rights.

Electoral reform

Representatives of smaller parties, such as the Green Party and the UK Independence Party, have won election to the European Parliament because the relationship between votes and seats is more proportional than before. The proportional voting system used for elections to the Scottish Parliament saw the Conservatives gain a fairer representation for their supporters (compared with the outcome of elections for Scottish constituencies in the House of Commons).

Assessment: criticism of Labour's reforms

There are two broad fronts of criticism directed at the reforms of Blair's Labour government: that the reforms are inadequate (from the Liberal Democrat perspective) and that the reforms have gone too far (traditionally, the Conservative view).

The reforms are inadequate

Devolution

Nationalist parties, such as the Scottish National Party (SNP), traditionally believe that nothing short of independence is necessary for Scotland. They have argued that, at the very least, the powers of the devolved Scottish Parliament should be enhanced to give the Scottish people more autonomy. Plaid Cymru in Wales has argued that the powers of the National Assembly for Wales are woefully inadequate and that Wales should have legislative and financial devolution, like Scotland.

Human rights legislation

Critics of the Human Rights Act (HRA), for example the pressure group Liberty, claim that the Act is too easy to amend and that citizens' rights are not sufficiently entrenched, when compared with the Bill of Rights of the US Constitution. The UK government has already amended the Human Rights Act to give itself extra powers against terrorists. It may be argued that the non-entrenched nature of the HRA could lead to other changes in the future that happen to coincide with the particular views of the government of the day. Key rights, such as freedom of expression and freedom of association, could be at threat. Indeed, it may be claimed that the use of national security as an excuse to curtail rights is made easier in a system that does not seek to entrench those rights in a codified constitution.

Electoral reform

Critics, such as the Liberal Democrats and members of groups such as the Electoral Reform Society and Charter 88, believe that proportional electoral systems should not be restricted to second-order elections, such as those to devolved bodies and the European Parliament. They insist that there should be electoral reform across all elections in the UK, including those to the House of Commons.

The reforms have gone too far

Devolution

Most Conservatives and some Labour critics of devolution warn that the process may lead to the eventual break up of the UK. Nationalists, for example, are already calling for devolved bodies to be given more power. This pressure may lead to the gradual transfer of powers away from London, after which a 'tipping point' will be reached.

Human rights legislation

Critics of the HRA claim that its introduction was unnecessary, in that the UK had long been regarded as a tolerant and respectful country where the rights of citizens were uncodified but well understood. They maintain that the HRA gives too much power to non-elected judges. Such power could be used to rule against democratically elected politicians. Furthermore, the HRA has created a culture of rights litigation in the UK, which could lead to a more divisive society, with certain social groups using the law and the courts to seek to raise their status.

Electoral reform

Critics of the reformed electoral system point to a number of problems, such as the MEP–constituent link being broken by the introduction of the party list electoral system.

UK political parties and constitutional reform

There are many political parties with views on the issue of constitutional reform. For the purposes of this unit test, you need examine only the standpoints of the three main parties. Clearly on the issue of devolution you need to be aware of the positions of the Scottish and Welsh nationalist parties.

The Conservatives

The Conservatives traditionally believe that there is no need to reform the constitution. They are against 'reform for reform's sake', seeing evolution of the constitution as preferable to revolution. In their view, the constitution should change only when there is an obvious problem and where a clear solution exists that will make things better.

They argue that Labour is guilty of vandalising the constitution and that devolution will lead to the break up of the UK. The Human Rights Act has given too much power to non-elected judges and tinkering with the electoral system will lead to weaker government, which they claim is already the case in Scotland and Wales.

At present, the Conservatives are in opposition and have to live with the changes introduced by Labour. This has been particularly difficult from the point of view of devolution, where there appear to be real divisions within the party over the issue. Many Scottish Conservatives have seen devolution revive the party's fortunes north of the border and are irritated by the continued opposition of many English Conservatives.

Labour

Labour made constitutional reform a major element of its manifesto in the 1997 general election, seeing it as part of its new agenda for the UK. Devolution in Scotland and Wales was a response to public opinion and expectations in those countries. Reform in Northern Ireland was, in the government's view, the only way to achieve peace in the province. Incorporating the European Convention of Human Rights through the Human Rights Act brought the UK into line with many other European countries, both inside and outside the European Union. Electoral reform is regarded by Labour as fairer and more democratic.

When in opposition, Labour had an understanding with the Liberal Democrats that the issue of constitutional reform would be taken seriously by an incoming Labour government. It would be an error, however, to suggest that the Labour Party is in favour of all constitutional reforms. Many at the top of the party are sceptical about reforming the voting system for elections to the House of Commons. Similarly, there are no calls from within the party for a fully codified constitution. Indeed, it is interesting to note that virtually all meaningful constitutional reforms were enacted during Labour's first term of office, 1997–2001.

Another aspect of Labour's attitude is that, having embarked upon a programme of constitutional reform at the same time as being in office for an extended period, there now appears to be a reluctance within the party to give up any more of its power. This can be seen in its handling of House of Lords reform, as well as in its decision to stall reform of elections to the House of Commons.

The Liberal Democrats

The Liberal Democrats have a long-held commitment to radical constitutional reform. This is hardly surprising since, in the past, Liberal Democrat candidates have been some of the highest-profile casualties of the first-past-the-post voting system. Nationally, the party has polled millions of votes at general elections in return for only small numbers of seats in the House of Commons.

The party's commitment to devolution is well known. During the 1990s and in the run up to the 1997 general election, the Liberal Democrats developed a joint policy with the Labour Party, which was to be the blueprint for the eventual devolution plans of the Blair government. After the 1997 general election, the Liberal Democrat leader and a number of other senior figures from the party were invited onto a cabinet sub-committee working on various aspects of constitutional reform. This was the first time in more than 50 years that the third party in UK politics had found itself working within the machinery of government. The policies they were working on were some of those closest to the hearts of many Liberal Democrats.

The case for adopting a codified constitution in the UK

Many members of the Liberal Democrats and pressure groups such as Charter 88 are in favour of a full, codified constitution, along the lines of the US and German constitutions. They argue that a codified constitution would:

- Reduce the dominance of the executive in UK politics. The powers of individual political institutions would be clearly defined, with precise limits imposed if necessary.
- Clearly lay out the powers of the various parts of the political system, regulating the way that these institutions interrelate. In the USA, the powers of the president in relationship to the Supreme Court, for example, are laid down in a single document. Similarly, the division of responsibilities between federal and state authorities are also specified.
- Ensure adequate protection of the rights of citizens. Within such a document it is possible to enshrine and safeguard such rights more easily and thereby protect them from easy amendment.

The case against adopting a codified constitution in the UK

Opponents of a codified constitution, on both the right and left of the political spectrum, warn of:

- The danger of handing more political power to the judiciary. A US-style Supreme Court could see unaccountable judges straying into the political arena. Indeed, many recent senior judicial appointments in the USA point to this being a concern of some presidents.
- Loss of political accountability. It is argued that a codified constitution would see less power being wielded by elected politicians and more political judgements being made in courts.
- The relative rigidity of a codified constitution when compared with an uncodified one. The UK would lose its flexible and adaptable constitution if it took on a codified model.
- Losing a tried and tested model. The UK constitution has evolved over centuries and is best fitted to the country. Many of the central aspects of the political order (parliamentary sovereignty, for example) would be lost if the system were reformed in such a way.

Parliament

Parliament is the legislative branch of the political system in the United Kingdom. In other words, it is the legislature or the place where laws are made. Parliament is composed of three parts:

- the monarch
- the House of Lords
- the House of Commons

Technically, the **monarch** has the final say as to whether a bill can pass into law by giving it royal assent, after which the bill becomes an Act of Parliament. However, no monarch has declined to give the royal assent to a bill since Queen Anne, who died in 1714.

The **House of Lords** has the power to delay legislation, although, as was seen on the issue of hunting with dogs, parliamentary devices exist to enable the House of Commons to get its own way. The Lords is a deliberative and revising chamber.

It is the **House of Commons** that has the greatest influence. It is where every prime minister of the past century has sat and over 90% of all ministers are drawn from it. When discussing the power of Parliament, much emphasis is placed on the role of the House of Commons, especially its relationship to the executive.

Parliamentary government

The United Kingdom has a fusion of powers unlike in the United States, for example, which has a separation of powers (see pages 12–13). In other words, in the UK the legislative and executive branches of the constitution are fused or joined together.

The best way to describe the relationship between the legislative branch (Parliament) and the executive branch (government) is by use of the three prepositions 'in', 'through' and 'to':

- **in** — the executive is **in** the legislature, in that all members of the executive are drawn from either the House of Commons or the House of Lords
- **through** — government legislation must pass **through** and be approved by Parliament
- **to** — government is accountable **to** Parliament via a number of methods (such as questions to ministers)

Comparison with presidential government

In a presidential system of government, such as in the United States, there is no fusion of powers. Presidential government is based upon the separation of powers of the legislature and the executive. The president is not accountable to the legislature (Congress in the US), but is elected directly by voters. There is no equivalent in the United States of the weekly Prime Minister's Question Time, and the only way that Congress can rid itself of a president is by impeachment for 'high crimes and misdemeanours'. That, as was seen with President Clinton in the late 1990s, is a difficult task to undertake. Indeed, only two other US presidents have faced trials of impeachment, and neither of these attempts to remove the president was successful.

Parliamentary sovereignty

Parliamentary sovereignty is the centrally accepted convention of the constitution in the UK. Parliament is technically the supreme law-making body, and no other body can ultimately override its decisions. Parliament cannot be bound by the decisions of previous parliaments, and all other parts of the constitution (common law, for example) can be changed by Parliament. Parliament can reverse any decision that may have ceded power elsewhere, such as to the devolved assemblies in Scotland, Wales, Northern Ireland and the European Union. Parliament is only subject to the political sovereignty of the people at the time of a general election.

But parliamentary sovereignty may be said to be limited in a number of ways; both internal and external factors may be identified. Internally, ministers increasingly tend to conduct activities away from Parliament, where their activities could be scrutinised effectively. The creation of quangos and executive agencies, arguably, has made ministers less accountable to Parliament. The creation of devolved institutions, while not officially shifting sovereignty, has led to further powers being handed over, and despite the formal constitutional position, realistically it would be difficult for Parliament to reclaim those powers.

External factors include the powers of the institutions of the European Union and the various treaty obligations that the country has to international organisations (such as the North Atlantic Treaty Organisation, NATO). The power of transnational companies and financial institutions could also be cited as a limitation on Parliament's ability to exercise its sovereignty. Again, in theory it would be possible for Parliament to revoke any of its treaty obligations, but this is not very likely. In this respect, it may be useful to distinguish between formal sovereignty and effective sovereignty.

EU membership has affected the UK constitution in a number of respects. Most important is the impact it has had on parliamentary sovereignty, a fundamental element of the British constitution that many believe has been eroded by EU membership. On signing up to the EEC in 1973, the UK inherited 43 volumes of European legislation and 3,000 directives and regulations already in force elsewhere in the community. The UK Parliament, once able to pass any law it wished, became subject to the primacy of European law, meaning that the UK could be taken to the European Court of Justice if it was seen to be in contravention of European law.

The UK Parliament can no longer claim to be the ultimate power in the land. Where UK law and European law clash, the latter has primacy. The position of the judiciary has consequently been brought into focus, in that judges must now favour European law where it conflicts with UK law. This relationship was exemplified in the *Factortame* case of 1991, when part of the UK's merchant shipping legislation was struck down after it was declared contrary to European law.

While it might be argued that pooling of sovereignty across the EU could make the UK stronger, not weaker, there is no doubt that the nation's sovereignty has come under attack to such an extent as to question its status in the twenty-first century. That said, it should be stressed that in the main areas of public policy, member states still retain substantial control. The UK, for example, has control over immigration policy and national border controls (unlike a number of other EU member states). Powers over tax and general economic policy, defence and foreign policy are also retained by each individual EU member state.

Finally, of course, it is still possible for the UK to rescind the treaties that have been ratified over the years and withdraw from the EU entirely. However, many believe that the political and economic costs of doing so would be too great to consider such a move.

Impact of devolution

Between 1997 and 2001, devolved assemblies in Scotland, Wales and Northern Ireland were established. These assemblies have taken over complete control of services such as education in their respective areas. In the case of Scotland and Northern Ireland, the devolved bodies have primary legislative powers, in other words the power to make law. Furthermore, Scotland has tax-varying powers.

It may be claimed that the impact of devolution has been to reduce the power of Parliament and effectively to transfer sovereignty to the devolved assemblies. Strictly speaking there has been no formal transfer of sovereignty, but the extent to which Parliament remains sovereign would be tested if there were ever a move to reduce the powers of the devolved bodies or to abolish them altogether. It seems unlikely that the Westminster Parliament could do this, if public opinion in, for instance, Scotland were utterly opposed to it. A conflict could escalate into a constitutional crisis and this could potentially lead to a majority of Scots wishing to leave the United Kingdom.

Another contentious issue is the West Lothian Question, named after the poser of the question, Tam Dalyell, who was the MP for the Scottish constituency of West Lothian when he opposed Scottish devolution in the late 1970s. Dalyell questioned whether, with devolution, it was right that MPs elected to the House of Commons from Scottish constituencies should be able to vote on issues solely affecting England. MPs representing English constituencies would not have the right to influence similar issues in Scotland or Wales, because these powers would have been devolved to the Scottish Parliament and the Welsh Assembly respectively.

Arguably, with the passing of the Scotland Act in 1998 and the creation of the Scottish Parliament in 1999, Tam Dalyell's prediction has come about. Although there has been no attempt by the government to deal with this anomaly (for example, by removing the power of Scottish MPs to vote on exclusively English matters), there has been some recognition that perhaps the Scottish are over-represented in the House of Commons; in the 2005 general election, the number of Scottish constituencies (and therefore Scottish MPs) was reduced by 13, from 72 to 59. The issue remained alive, however, with the Conservatives wanting to see MPs from Scottish constituencies banned from voting on English-only matters.

Supporters of devolution, however, see benefits accruing to the Westminster Parliament. They see devolution as a more logical way of overseeing the legal and educational systems of Scotland, which have, in the past, required separate legislative time in any case. It may even be argued that devolution relieves some of the workload of the House of Commons, freeing it to concentrate on important issues and to deal with the needs of England.

Composition of Parliament

House of Commons

The House of Commons is composed of 646 members, each of whom is the representative of a constituency. At the dissolution of Parliament in April 2005, apart from the speaker, all but one of those MPs was a member of a political party (the exception was Dr Richard Taylor, MP for Wyre Forest, who stood in the 2001 general election as an independent candidate).

The constituency of each Member of Parliament is a geographical area which contains on average 60,000 electors. The exact number varies from one constituency to another, because in some of the more sparsely populated areas, such as northern Scotland, constituencies could become physically too large for a single MP to represent effectively.

Each MP has been elected by at least a plurality of votes in his or her constituency, and serves for a maximum of 5 years before seeking re-election or retirement. On the death or resignation of an MP between general elections, a writ is issued for a by-election to be held and a new MP is elected to represent the constituency for the remainder of the parliamentary term.

House of Lords

Unlike the Commons, the House of Lords is not elected and is composed instead of different types of lords (peers):

- **Hereditary peers** are those who have inherited their positions from their parents. At one time this was the biggest group in the Lords, accounting for over 600 members (although few used to attend for debates in the chamber). Since reforms made in 1999, only 92 hereditary peers remain.
- **Life peers**, under the Life Peerages Act 1958, are ennobled for the remainder of their lifetimes and their titles die with them. This was an attempt to breathe life into the House of Lords at a time when it was under fire from the left and centre. Life peers are appointed because they have proved to be successful in their chosen fields of politics, education, science, business or industry.
- **Law Lords** are the senior judges (such as the Lord Chief Justice and the Master of the Rolls) who sit as the highest judicial court in the land.
- **Bishops** are the senior archbishops and bishops of the Church of England.

It may be noted that lords occupy their position because of either birth, job or status. As mentioned above, some changes have already been introduced to reform the nature of the House of Lords, but this is a job only half-finished and there remains a debate about the future of the second chamber — whether it should be fully or partially elected, or whether it should remain an unelected body.

Functions of Parliament

Debating major issues

Parliament is the place where people expect issues of major importance to be discussed. For example, the House of Commons held debates before the war in Iraq. Parliament becomes the focus of the nation's attention on these occasions. If a crisis emerges during a parliamentary recess, it is not unusual for members to demand that Parliament be recalled in order for the issue to be discussed.

Making law (legislating)

All government legislation must pass through what can be a lengthy set of stages in both the House of Commons and the House of Lords before it reaches the statute book. This gives members the opportunity to debate the principles of the bill before them as well as the detail of the legislation. There is also the opportunity for MPs to table amendments to the legislation in order to get concessions from the government. Delegated legislation does not have to pass through a rigorous procedure, but orders still have to be laid before MPs.

Scrutinising the executive

This is perhaps the most important function of Parliament, especially at a time when the government has a great deal of power. Parliament scrutinises government in a number of ways which are discussed on pages 33–34.

Sustaining government

The United Kingdom has a system of parliamentary government, so, as well as holding the government to account, Parliament should also ensure that the government can actually govern. This is achieved by the governing party having a majority of seats in the House of Commons.

Representation

One of the key functions of Parliament is to represent the people. Political parties attempt to reflect the views of the people who elect them. Individual MPs attempt to represent the people in their constituency, whether they voted for them or not. In this way MPs are accountable. There is a discussion about how representative Parliament is overleaf.

Financial scrutiny

A key function of the Commons is the scrutiny of public spending. There is an annual Finance Bill, otherwise known as the Budget, which has to be passed in order for taxation and spending to continue. In addition, there are a number of parliamentary committees that oversee matters such as government spending. In this way, Parliament can be said to have ongoing control of public finances.

Redress of grievances

Historically, one of the earliest purposes of the Commons was for people to obtain redress for problems and grievances. Centuries later, citizens can still go to Parliament and lobby their MP about a particular issue that concerns them. Some MPs take up such causes and can either try to persuade government to change the law or attempt to change the law themselves using the procedure of private members' legislation.

How effective is Parliament?

Representation

Parliament is representative in a number of respects:
- Each eligible voter has a choice of constituency representatives. The chosen representative should represent everyone in the constituency, not just those who voted for him or her. Nearly all MPs hold regular 'surgeries' in their constituencies, where constituents can ask for help with problems. This may lead to the MP asking a question to a minister on behalf of the constituent. Alternatively, constituents may travel to Westminster and lobby their MP.
- There is usually a good range of political parties from which to choose. It may be argued that the parties currently in the House of Commons represent a good cross-section of political opinion. At a general election, in most constituencies voters have a choice of at least three political parties, and usually five or six.
- Although Parliament is not a microcosm (small-scale version) of society, it may be argued that it broadly reflects the nation and takes into account the interests of minority groups that may be under-represented in Parliament. The extent to which these groups can be seen to be protected is illustrated by the passing of race relations legislation in the 1960s and 1970s at a time when there was not a single black or Asian MP.
- Parliament is usually responsive to public opinion. When the public mood is moved by an event, Parliament can be quick to take these feelings into account. After the mass shooting of children at a primary school in Dunblane in 1996, Parliament moved quickly to tighten the law on gun ownership. It could be argued that Parliament is sometimes overly responsive, however. Many commentators agree that Parliament rushed to judgement too quickly when it passed the Dangerous Dogs Act after a number of highly publicised attacks by dogs on young children.

There are also a number of arguments that Parliament is not sufficiently representative in certain key respects:
- In the House of Commons, certain groups of people are not properly represented. Despite increased numbers in recent years, women account for fewer than one-sixth of MPs. Others, such as those from ethnic groups, are similarly under-represented (although this may be more to do with party selection procedures than any fault of Parliament itself).
- Political parties are represented in a disproportionate manner. Under the 'first-past-the-post' electoral system, parties do not usually gain seats in the House of Commons in proportion to their support in the popular vote. Traditionally, the Liberal Democrats and other smaller parties have been hit hard in this respect. More recently, however, the Conservatives have also found themselves to be under-represented by over 50 seats in proportion to their percentage of the vote,

after the general elections of 1997 and 2001. The workings of the British electoral system prevent some parties, such as the Green Party and the UK Independence Party, from being represented at all in the House of Commons.

- The House of Lords has been criticised because it is an unelected chamber. Until recently, most peers were hereditary and therefore not representative of the country politically, socially, economically or by gender or ethnic origin. Most peers are now nominated, which it is argued does not necessarily improve the House's representativeness.

Scrutiny of the executive

There are a number of ways in which Parliament scrutinises the work of government:

Questions to ministers

Departments take turns to answer parliamentary questions. Question Time takes place from Monday to Thursday for 1 hour each day. On Wednesdays, the prime minister answers questions for half of the hour-long slot.

MPs with questions submit their names to the speaker in advance. Ministers need to be well briefed on the topics likely to arise, especially if a relevant issue has arisen in the news in recent days.

There are oral questions and written questions. The idea of Question Time is that the opposition may seek out flaws in government policy, but also individual MPs may obtain useful information for their constituents.

Debates

Debates are discussions, and in Parliament they are the method of putting views across as well as opening the government to criticism. If legislation has not been well thought through or a lack of planning is evident in a government proposal, an exchange on the floor of the Commons or the Lords can make this plain for all to see. It is for this reason that the government employs large numbers of parliamentary draftsmen to ensure that legislation is in robust shape before going through its stages in the Commons and the Lords.

Select committees

These committees were first introduced in 1979, and were modelled on the select committees that work in the US Congress. They are responsible for scrutinising the work of individual government departments. The committees are cross-party, although their composition does reflect the strength of party support in the House of Commons. They investigate issues to do with the department that they scrutinise. They interview ministers, civil servants and other individuals who might help with their work. They publish reports and make recommendations to the government.

Opposition days

These are so called because they are days that 'belong' to the opposition. Normally it is the government side of the Commons that determines the daily timetable in the chamber, and this is usually focused upon moving legislation forwards. There are a limited number of days, however, that the official opposition can use. They need to give notice of their intention to use such a day, and normally reserve them for issues that might be embarrassing to the government.

Limitations to scrutiny

It may be argued that in a number of respects these mechanisms for scrutiny are not totally effective in ensuring that the executive is held to account by Parliament. Parliament encounters a number of problems in scrutinising the executive:

- Scrutiny is made difficult if one party dominates the House of Commons. In the mid to late 1980s, the Conservatives dominated the Commons, and between 1997 and 2005, Labour enjoyed even greater control. It is very difficult to hold government to account when so many MPs are sitting on the governing party's benches in the Commons chamber.
- Question Time is not usually a very effective form of scrutiny. Many commentators agree that it often 'generates more heat than light'. The tribal instincts of MPs make it more likely that they will rally around the party leadership, and it is rare for MPs to inflict damaging blows at Question Time. By contrast to oral questions, tabled on the floor of the House of Commons, written questions to ministers are often more fruitful. This might be to do with the fact that written questions tend not to open ministers to too much public attention and potential embarrassment.
- When it comes to debating legislation, many MPs lack the technical expertise or the interest to scrutinise adequately bills going through the Commons. Real scrutiny often relies on those MPs who have particular areas of interest or expertise. While in opposition, the Labour MP Frank Field, who before his parliamentary career had been head of the Child Poverty Action Group, took a keen interest in welfare matters. Field was skilled in the policy detail going through Parliament. Most MPs neither possess nor wish to possess such skills.
- Poor timing of opposition days may blunt their impact. There is the temptation not to use up these days in case a major political controversy erupts. As a consequence, the opposition may come to the end of a parliamentary session and still have days to use, but no issue with which to stir up publicity and government discomfort. Conversely, even on a major issue, the reality of opposition days often does not match the expectation generated beforehand.
- Some select committees do not exert their independence as effectively as others. Select committees are composed in a way that reflects the representation of the political parties in the Commons. Needless to say, Labour MPs have dominated these committees for much of the past decade. It is generally agreed that the most effective select committees are those that try to reach conclusions that have cross-party support, rather than those whose reports tend to be highly partisan.

Parliamentary reform

There have been a number of reforms in both houses of Parliament. The most commented upon have been those to the House of Lords. Perhaps it might be appropriate to begin by looking at some of the changes that have been made to the workings of the House of Commons.

The House of Commons

The changes to the Commons are, on the whole, non-structural. They cannot, for example, be compared with the introduction of the departmental select committee system at the start of the Thatcher government in May 1979. Almost as soon as the Blair government took office, Prime Minister's Question Time was modified from two 15-minute slots per week to the current one 30-minute slot every Wednesday. In addition, the prime minister made himself available for questions twice a year before the House of Commons Liaison Committee. After the 1997 general election, in an attempt to accommodate the large influx of women MPs and to make the working day of Parliament more family-friendly, the government stopped the late-night sittings of the Commons (though MPs have recently voted to reinstate them).

The House of Lords

Probably the most debated aspect of parliamentary reform is that of the House of Lords, which remains a totally non-elected second chamber. What changes have been introduced so far and what are the main arguments surrounding the second chamber becoming elected or partially elected?

Reforms enacted so far

The Labour Party has long called for reform of the House of Lords. Labour MPs partic- ularly have resented their legitimate authority being challenged by non-elected peers who are accountable to no one. The Blair government moved to cut the number of hereditary peers down to 92 as part of a reform bill introduced in 1999, but many Labour backbenchers expected much swifter and more decisive measures and were disappointed by the government's response.

Future plans

As part of a longer-term settlement, the Blair government asked former Conservative chief whip John Wakeham to investigate possible future models for the second chamber. His report, published in 2000, drew on a number of models of varying combi- nations of elected and non-elected (nominated) members. Wakeham concluded that a second chamber, largely non-elected but with some elected members, should replace the House of Lords.

Initially, the government did nothing in response to the Wakeham Report. Then, in 2003, a number of proposals for reform were put before both houses of Parliament. None of these received majority support. By the time of the 2005 general election, there was still no clear indication of how the government intended to proceed. The Labour Party manifesto stated simply that in the next term they would complete the reform process 'so that it is a modern and effective revising chamber' (Labour Party Manifesto 2005, p.102). At the time of writing, there are no specific proposals for further reform, but there is much talk of an elected element to the second chamber.

In February 2007, the government published a White Paper declaring its future intentions for the reform of the second chamber. These included a commitment to abolish the 92 remaining hereditary peers. The following month the House of Commons voted for an entirely elected second chamber. A week later the House of Lords voted for an all-appointed second chamber. The government of Gordon Brown has signalled that it wishes to complete the process of second chamber reform. In May 2008, Brown announced that the government would publish another White Paper on reform of the House of Lords.

Criticisms of the Lords reforms

As usual, when it comes to discussing actual (rather than theoretical) constitutional reform, there have been criticisms. Groups such as Charter 88 consider the reforms to be insufficiently robust, and groups on the right of the political spectrum believe that the reforms go too far.

Insufficiently robust

Many of those in favour of more radical reforms to the House of Lords argue that there should be a fully elected Parliament, which would be more democratic and accountable to the people. Another view is that the second chamber should be abolished and the UK should retain a **unicameral legislature**, like Israel (see below).

Going too far

Other criticisms come from those who believe that the reforms have gone too far. One argument is that Parliament functions perfectly well as it is and should be left alone. It has, in any case, the ability to make adjustments to itself without undertaking reform. There is also the risk of losing well-established practices, which have worked in the past, in the pursuit of solving relatively minor difficulties. It could be argued that, during the 1980s, it was the unreformed House of Lords that frequently proved to be a more effective check on the Thatcher government than the Labour opposition of the time.

The Conservatives, long seen as the party of caution when it comes to matters involving constitutional reform, have been critical of the changes made to the House of Lords so far. It could be argued, of course, that they would be bound to oppose any policy that weakened their position in Westminster (most hereditary peers were Conservative), especially in view of the weakness of their position in the Commons.

Should the Lords be elected?

Arguments in favour of a fully elected second chamber are:
- It would be more democratic.
- It would add legitimacy to the political process, i.e. if both chambers were elected, there would be no question over whether legislation had the consent of the people.
- It would make all legislators responsive to the mood of the public and accountable to them at the time of an election.
- It would provide the country with a modern revising chamber fit for the twenty-first century.

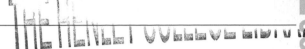

Arguments against a fully elected second chamber are:

- The present situation in the Lords is just about acceptable, in that most of the hereditary peers have now gone (they were the biggest point of contention as far as the second chamber was concerned).
- There is the potential for gridlock between the two elected chambers each time a disagreement has to be resolved.
- Lord Wakeham himself questioned the calibre of members that could be recruited if the powers of an elected second chamber were contrived to wield minimum influence.
- The loss of nominated life peers would deny the political system the valuable contributions to the legislative process made by some experienced and successful individuals.
- Some of the finest parliamentary committees (such as the House of Lords European Committee) would also be lost.

Abolishing the second chamber

As mentioned above, there is a minority of opinion that favours having a single chamber in Parliament, the so-called **unicameral option**. This proposal would remove the decision-making process from non-elected people, without the need to introduce a second chamber and the associated risks of political gridlock.

Opponents of this idea argue that the volume of work done by Parliament necessitates two chambers. Furthermore, not having a second chamber to deliberate and revise the work of the first might lead to the passing of ill-thought-out and hastily discussed legislation, which could lead to bad law.

The Conservatives' position reassessed

In recent years, the Conservative Party has undergone a major change of policy on the issue of parliamentary reform. From being implacably opposed to reforming the Lords, the party has now modified its stance. In 2002, the Conservative leader, Iain Duncan Smith, unveiled a policy supporting a new second chamber — a slimmed-down senate that would be fully elected. His successor, Michael Howard, remained in line with this policy up until the 2005 general election. Howard's successor, David Cameron, has made similar commitments to the idea of an elected second chamber.

Party politics could, of course, have played their part here. Blair's government had been in some discomfort over what to do about the second stage of House of Lords reform. This new Conservative policy could have been designed to maximise Blair's difficulties with his own backbenchers, who would probably have been more sympathetic to an elected second chamber than their leader.

The executive

For the purposes of AS study, it is sufficient to understand the executive as being another word for the government. In the United Kingdom, the government is made up of a number of principal elements, including the prime minister, the cabinet, ministers outside the cabinet and civil servants.

Formation of the executive

One of the key features of the UK political system is that there is parliamentary government — in other words, members of the government are also members of Parliament. The prime minister and other ministers are directly elected by voters in their respective constituencies, but they are elected as MPs and not as ministers. A general election is where all the constituencies select their MPs for seats in the House of Commons. Whichever political party wins over half of these 646 seats wins the general election and becomes the governing party.

The leader of the winning party is summoned by the monarch and is made prime minister. He or she then appoints other ministers inside and outside the cabinet. Normally the prime minister is appointed on the day after the election, and within a couple of days all cabinet ministers and most of the other ministers are in post.

This contrasts with the formation of the executive in the United States, where the president is directly elected in early November but does not take up the job until the end of January. Furthermore, none of the president's ministers are members of either house of the US Congress.

The position of prime minister

The prime minister is sometimes described using the Latin phrase *primus inter pares*, in other words 'first among equals'. The prime minister is literally first in the sense that he or she is the first minister in the government to be appointed, as mentioned above. The prime minister is also first in the sense of being the most important minister in the government, and although 'first among equals' is something of a contradiction, the phrase tries to convey the meaning of the prime minister's position. Essentially, government in the UK is a collective enterprise with a single head to guide it.

The prime minister's sources of power

Appointment and patronage

The prime minister is responsible for the selection of cabinet and non-cabinet ministers. As mentioned above, this is one of the first tasks that the prime minister has to undertake. Furthermore, throughout their time in office prime ministers periodically promote and dismiss ministers, as well as dealing with vacancies arising from ministerial resignations. This power is significant in the sense that ambitious backbench MPs know that their careers will depend to a large extent on their loyalty to the government and ultimately to the prime minister. Within government, ministers appreciate that future promotion may also depend on the loyalty they display.

The prime minister also has the power to appoint people outside the government. The appointment of the chair of the BBC is subject to the ultimate agreement of the prime minister. In addition, hundreds of places on government-appointed quangos are, ultimately, in the gift of the prime minister. Until recently, the prime minister was also responsible for the appointment of new members of the House of Lords. At the moment an independent appointments body oversees this process, but the prime minister still has some control over a number of appointments, as well as appointments to the body itself.

The royal prerogative

Most of the powers that are exercised by the prime minister derive from the royal prerogative — powers that have traditionally been dispensed by the monarch. As time has gone by, these powers have effectively moved into the hands of the prime minister.

Officially, it is the monarch who dissolves Parliament, which then forces a general election. In practice, however, the prime minister asks for a dissolution of Parliament when he or she wants a general election to be held.

Another power derived from the royal prerogative is the power to declare war. Although it is done in the name of the monarch, this decision is usually taken by the prime minister. Interestingly, in the case of the war in Iraq in 2003, Tony Blair took the issue to a debate in the House of Commons for a decision to be made. Even before he became prime minister, Gordon Brown indicated that Parliament should be consulted before any future commitment to go to war.

Majority

The prime minister commands a majority of MPs in the House of Commons. It may be argued that the bigger the majority, the greater the power. It is interesting to contrast the premiership of John Major, who for most of his time in office had a small or no Commons majority, with that of his predecessor Margaret Thatcher, or his successor Tony Blair. A majority in Parliament enables the prime minister to get most if not all legislation through the Commons. Despite numerous backbench revolts, Tony Blair did not suffer a single Commons defeat between 1997 and 2005.

Party

Since the mid-1960s, all prime ministers have been the elected leaders of their political parties. The parties have different systems for choosing their leaders, but ultimately it is the party that can get rid of them. Parties normally remain loyal to their leaders, but if events dictate, this loyalty can disappear. Margaret Thatcher was forced out because the Parliamentary Conservative Party, who at that time decided the leadership issue, failed to support her in sufficient numbers when she was challenged for the position by Michael Heseltine.

Personality

In an age when the media concentrate heavily on the personalities of politicians, the focus of attention is often on the leaders of the major political parties, and in particular on the prime minister. During the general election campaigns of 1997 and 2001, much emphasis was placed on Tony Blair himself. His face appeared prominently on the cover of Labour's party manifesto in both of these general elections. A leader who can display a strong and popular personality, coupled with the other factors mentioned above, can prove to be a powerful holder of the office. It could be argued that one of the main problems faced by Gordon Brown has been his inability to project a media image that is attractive to the public.

Factors constraining the prime minister's power

Factors affecting appointments

Colleagues who have shown support and personal loyalty to the prime minister will expect some reward. If loyalty is not seen to be rewarded, then one reason for displaying political loyalty, self-interest, will weaken. This is particularly important during times of political difficulty for the government. Michael Heseltine was made deputy prime minister in 1995, in what was seen as a reward for unstinting support of John Major in his fight for the Conservative Party leadership.

There may be occasions when it is politically astute to have critics within the government. It is often better to keep potentially troublesome colleagues off the backbenches and inside the government, where they would be expected to maintain support of government policy. It may be argued that Tony Benn remained in the cabinet in the 1970s, in spite of his disagreements with both prime ministers Harold Wilson and James Callaghan, because of this factor. More recently, Gordon Brown ensured that former Blair loyalists such as John Hutton were given positions in government. Similarly, it can be better to keep potential rivals inside the cabinet. It may be argued, however, that David Miliband was given a top ministerial position (foreign secretary) for not standing against Gordon Brown for the Labour leadership in 2007.

The prime minister may wish to have a balance of opinions within the party in government. Clare Short could not have been described as a keen advocate of the so-called 'middle way', yet she became an important figure in Tony Blair's cabinet until her resignation in 2003. Although the Blair government lost most, if not all, advocates of 'old Labour', the continued presence of Gordon Brown showed that there was an alternative to the Blair agenda at the core of the Labour Party. It is interesting to note, however, that much of Brown's newness as a prime minister has been about style rather than policy substance.

The expectations of certain individuals may also be a constraining factor on appointments. Some colleagues may justifiably expect to be included in the government, and some may expect a particular job. In 1997, there was little doubt that on winning the general election Tony Blair would make Gordon Brown the chancellor of the exchequer; such was the standing of the latter in the party. Ten years later, it was no secret that Alistair Darling expected to be elevated to this position, and on the appointment of Gordon Brown as prime minister, he duly was.

Indeed the Labour Party has rules which effectively determine the choice of cabinet colleagues after first winning power. When in opposition, the shadow cabinet was elected by Labour MPs and Tony Blair was limited in his choice of colleagues immediately after the 1997 general election. Within a year, however, Blair had held his first cabinet reshuffle when a number of these people elected by MPs were sacked.

The prime minister is also expected to take account of gender and ethnic factors. By 2005, Tony Blair's cabinet contained five women and Paul Boateng, the first black MP to be appointed to the cabinet. In addition, there needs to be a balance of youth and experience, ensuring that younger MPs can build up their political careers. Gordon Brown's first cabinet contained six women, one of whom, Jacqui Smith, was the first woman home secretary.

Other constraints

All the sources of prime-ministerial power can also be seen as constraints. The parliamentary majority enjoyed by the prime minister's party may not be large. John Major won the 1992 general election with a modest majority, which placed his government in some difficulty with contentious legislation (such as the ratification of the Maastricht Treaty in 1992–93). Sometimes a government has no majority in Parliament and this can make its job more difficult, as James Callaghan found to his cost in the late 1970s. In the end he lost a vote of confidence in the House of Commons in 1979 and was forced to hold a general election, which was lost to Margaret Thatcher. Since 2005, both Tony Blair and Gordon Brown have had to lead governments with a significantly smaller majority of seats in the House of Commons.

The loyalty of the political party cannot always be assured. Margaret Thatcher herself led a party that was divided in loyalty in 1990 and eventually the cabinet forced her out during a leadership contest. John Major similarly had problems with certain parts of the Parliamentary Conservative Party, which undermined his authority in the eyes of the electorate. More recently, Tony Blair faced hostility from within his own party, particularly in the aftermath of the war in Iraq and concerning the pursuit of policies on tuition fees and foundation hospitals. Blair's final months as prime minister were characterised by backbench dissent. After an initial brief political honeymoon,

Gordon Brown is facing major criticisms from within the Labour Party about his abilities as prime minister.

The issue of personality is also double-edged. If the prime minister does not have much personal charisma, this can lead to a poor media image, which can be damaging. John Major and Gordon Brown have been said to lack the necessary personality and presence for the modern media age. Certainly when compared with Margaret Thatcher and Tony Blair this would seem to be the case. But these two prime ministers also suffered from political unpopularity. In the case of Margaret Thatcher it contributed to her downfall, because her party was nervous of defeat at the following general election. Tony Blair was more or less forced to announce his resignation a year in advance, due to backbench pressure.

The cabinet

The cabinet consists of only the most senior ministers in the government. Normally each government department has as its most senior minister a secretary of state who is a member of the cabinet — the secretary of state for health, for example, or the home secretary (whose proper title is the secretary of state for home affairs). Within government departments there are more junior ministers, such as under-secretaries of state or ministers of state, who are responsible for a particular part of the work of their department. These junior ministers are not in the cabinet.

Not all members of the cabinet are heads of government departments; some cabinet ministers have other, non-departmental responsibilities. They include the government chief whip and the leader of the House of Commons, as well as so-called ministers without portfolio, who may have some important party function.

Cabinet government

There are a number of theories about the role of the cabinet. Traditionally, the cabinet was seen as the heart of the policy-making process, a place of immense power and authority. Recently, however, more modest claims have been made about the cabinet's role.

The cabinet now meets only once a week and for less than an hour. It is difficult to conceive that a body that meets for so little time can really have a grip on the political system. In reality, the cabinet acts as a final nod to policy and often simply endorses the recommendations of other forums, such as cabinet sub-committees.

Where there is a breakdown in consensus between ministers, it is often the cabinet that collectively attempts to overcome any particular log-jam. In this respect, the cabinet, which has to be seen to be united in public (see below), performs a very useful task.

In spite of the tendency in recent decades for power within the cabinet to shift towards the prime minister and a cabal of favoured ministers and political advisers, there have been notable occasions where the collective has prevailed. Most notably, Margaret Thatcher resigned once she realised that she did not have the support of a significant proportion of her cabinet. Both Tony Blair and Gordon Brown have faced cabinet dissent in recent years.

Functions of the cabinet

In the past, at least, the cabinet was seen to be a central and crucially important part of the British political system. More recently, however, a number of commentators have questioned the importance of the cabinet in the decision-making process. One of the reasons for this is the rise in power of the prime minister, which has left unanswered the questions as to what the cabinet actually does and how powerful and important it is.

Most government and politics textbooks identify the following key functions of the cabinet:

Policy formulation

In theory, the cabinet should be at the heart of the policy-formulation process. Indeed, much policy does appear to spring from the cabinet. In reality, however, detailed policy formulation, discussion and implementation do not take place in the cabinet itself; there is neither the time nor the expertise around the cabinet table to do such tasks justice. Cabinet is often the place where policies may be prioritised or where other groups are mandated to undertake more detailed policy formulation.

Dealing with crises and emergencies

The cabinet plays an important role when unexpected events arise; cabinet ministers play an important part in presenting a united face in confronting a national crisis. After so-called 'Black Wednesday' in September 1992, when the UK was forced out of the European exchange rate mechanism (ERM), the entire cabinet met to endorse the economic policy of the government and to show solidarity with the prime minister and the chancellor of the exchequer.

Controlling the parliamentary agenda

There is a finite amount of time in which to debate various government policies in Parliament, and the cabinet is responsible for prioritising the business of Parliament. In this respect, ministers are involved in a competitive struggle to get the policies of their departments turned into laws.

Ratifying decisions formulated elsewhere

In some respects the cabinet may be seen as an endorsing body. With much policy being formulated by cabinet committees, government departments or by other ad-hoc or informal groups, the cabinet is left with the task of endorsing or rejecting policy proposals.

Settling interdepartmental disputes

Government departments often compete for scarce resources and the allocation of time to get legislation onto the statute book. If an argument about this or any other matter cannot be settled bilaterally between the departments concerned, then the cabinet as a whole has the task of imposing a collective decision on those involved. On a number of occasions during the 1980s, the Thatcher cabinet was called upon to settle departmental disputes over the allocation of money for public expenditure.

Cabinet committees

The cabinet is divided into numerous sub-committees which look in greater detail at specific policy areas — there is an economic strategy committee, for example. These committees are composed of government ministers and civil servants. It is often at committee level that much of the formulation of government policy takes place.

Tony Blair has been criticised for downgrading the role of the cabinet; Margaret Thatcher was accused of doing the same. John Major, however, was credited with restoring the authority of the cabinet when he was prime minister between 1990 and 1997. Gordon Brown, speaking on the steps of 10 Downing Street on the day he took office in June 2007, declared that he wanted to restore the collective government of the cabinet.

Tony Blair reduced considerably the time that the cabinet meets. As mentioned above, it now meets for less than an hour a week. He seemed to prefer the bilateral approach when dealing with his ministers: in other words, one-on-one meetings. This ensures that focused discussions take place, and that there can be a proper and ongoing review of the work of individual government departments. Critics argue, however, that this approach gives the prime minister more influence over individual goverment departments.

Collective ministerial responsibility

Overall responsibility for the actions of the government is taken collectively by the whole government. Members of the cabinet and other government ministers must agree, in public at least, on government policy, and if a minister cannot agree with the collective decision of the cabinet, he or she must resign. There have been a number of instances of ministers resigning because of such disagreements. Just before the Iraq war in 2003, Robin Cook resigned from the cabinet because of his opposition to the UK's involvement in the invasion. Just after the Iraq war, Clare Short also resigned because of her unease with the way the United Nations' role in postwar Iraq was being marginalised by the United States.

Individual ministerial responsibility

Ministers are responsible for what happens in their own departments or sections within their departments. Ministers are expected to take the blame for mistakes made, and must answer publicly for their actions. They face regular questioning in the House of Commons and at select committee hearings, where they have to explain aspects of policy or procedure. Nowadays, the media subject ministers to additional scrutiny.

Traditionally, ministers are expected to resign if necessary, although for many years there were few examples of this happening. One such example was Lord Carrington's resignation as foreign secretary in 1982 because of Foreign Office failings in the period leading up to Argentina's invasion of the Falkland Islands. However, ministers have tried to do whatever they can to avoid resignation, even if that involves blaming other individuals within their departments. Most ministerial resignations over the past 20 years have had more to do with personal misconduct.

In the past few years, however, there have been a number of ministerial resignations which do appear to fit the theory of individual ministerial responsibility. In 2002, Stephen Byers resigned after what many regarded as a poor period as transport secretary. Later the same year, the education secretary Estelle Morris also resigned from the government, effectively admitting that she was not up to the job. In 2004, the immigration minister resigned because of a visa scam that had not been properly dealt with by the Home Office.

It may be argued that ministers try to avoid resigning after a problem arises in their department. Michael Howard faced down repeated calls for his resignation following a series of criticisms from members of the judiciary in the mid-1990s. Alistair Darling also resisted calls for his resignation over the government's handling of the Northern Rock crisis in late 2007.

In fact, ministers are nowadays as likely to resign due to personal misconduct as they are over political failures. The government of John Major was mired in allegations of sleaze in the years running up to the 1997 general election. Tony Blair also lost a number of trusted allies due to issues of conduct. Both Peter Mandelson and David Blunkett resigned twice from government over such issues.

Ministers and civil servants

Defining the civil service

Broadly, the function of the civil service is to advise and implement. The civil service includes routine clerical staff, executive staff (those who carry out policy), and advisory and decision-making staff. There are three constitutional principles that govern the workings of the UK civil service:

- **Permanence.** The civil service has traditionally been a career profession; in other words, civil servants remain in office even when a particular party loses power. For this reason they need to display the other two important characteristics.
- **Neutrality.** Civil servants must advise ministers and implement policy without bias or favour. They need to be able to do their jobs regardless of who is in power.
- **Anonymity.** Traditionally, civil servants have been expected to give ministers a range of advice, and this might involve the inclusion of controversial ideas. Ministers do not make this advice process public, since they must rely upon it in the future.

These three principles are tied in with an associated principle, that of individual ministerial responsibility. As noted above, ministers are expected to take responsibility for what happens in their departments. They take the praise when success is achieved; they must also take the blame when mistakes occur. When Lord Carrington resigned as foreign secretary in 1982 after the Argentine invasion of the Falkland Islands, it was clear that mistakes had been made at civil servant level; nonetheless, Lord Carrington believed that the responsibility was his and he resigned.

Ministers therefore have traditionally been unable to hide behind their civil servants. After all, it is ministers who are directly accountable to Parliament for the conduct of their departments, and the government that is ultimately collectively responsible.

Changes in the civil service

Some of the most important changes in the civil service have taken place since 1979. These have transformed the way civil servants operate, as well as the role that the civil service plays in the constitution. Some of these changes have been reforms, the two most important of which are the Rayner reforms and the Next Steps reforms.

Rayner reforms

After Margaret Thatcher was first elected in 1979, Marks and Spencer's boss Sir Derek Rayner was appointed to head an efficiency unit charged with ensuring that civil servants adopted a more businesslike approach in their departments. Phrases such as 'value for money' became more commonly used. Rayner wanted to cut out wasteful practices. He believed that this would make the civil service more efficient. Indeed, by the mid-1980s, the service saw a reduction in the number of civil servants from around 750,000 to about 600,000.

Next Steps reforms

Sir Derek Rayner was replaced by Sir Robin Ibbs in the mid-1980s. Ibbs wanted to take the issue of efficiency even further, by investigating how services were delivered. He argued that many of the functions of the civil service, such as the maintenance of roads and motorways or the payment of social security benefits, need not be controlled directly by the departments of transport or social security. Instead, they could be managed by dedicated 'agencies' that would deliver the service at arm's length from the government department. This would effectively separate the advisory/decision-making functions of the civil service from the implementation functions. By the end of the Major government in 1997 there were more than 130 of these executive agencies. Their number has continued to grow under Labour.

We are all familiar with bodies such as the Highways Agency, the Benefits Agency, the Driver and Vehicle Licensing Agency and the Environment Agency. These are all bodies whose functions at one time were being carried out from within government departments.

Political advisers

Perhaps one of the most controversial developments in recent years has been the growth in so-called special advisers. These are non-career civil servants who are appointed to offer political advice to ministers — advice likely to be in line with government policy. These advisers have been around for more than 40 years, but there was a big increase in their number after the 1997 general election. Now ministers have a number of sources of advice from within their departments.

How changes in the civil service have affected constitutional principles

Permanence in the civil service has been affected by the Rayner reforms, since many civil servants lost their jobs. The growth in the number of special advisers means that more civil servants leave their jobs when a minister leaves.

Neutrality has obviously been affected by the fact that there are now more partisan advisers taking civil service salaries. It should be pointed out, however, that the total number of special advisers is between 80 and 90, spread across all government departments. Given that there are well over half a million civil servants in total, the impact of these advisers on the principle of neutrality is not likely to be great.

Anonymity has been affected by the introduction of the departmental select committees in Parliament. Now civil servants and ministers may be summoned to give evidence to one of these committees — since their inception in 1979, many hundreds have been so summoned. The introduction of the Next Steps agencies has also made a difference to the principle of anonymity. Those individuals who are in charge of the agencies are much more likely to be in the public eye than their predecessors in the government departments.

Individual ministerial responsibility has also been influenced by some of these changes. The select committee system now exposes civil servants to the type of scrutiny that at one time only ministers faced in the chambers of the House of Commons and the House of Lords. Perhaps more significant has been the impact of the Next Steps reforms; it may be claimed that having divided policy and operational matters between the agency and the relevant department, ministers are now able to avoid responsibility for mistakes made at agency level. Perhaps the most vivid example of this was in the aftermath of a break-out by prisoners at Whitemoor Prison. The then home secretary sacked the head of the prison service, Derek Lewis, since it was considered to have been an operational error that had led to the escape.

The judiciary and civil liberties

Rights in Britain

Until the passing of the Human Rights Act in 1998, most (but not all) of the liberties enjoyed by citizens in the United Kingdom could only be expressed in negative terms. In other words, there were no laws declaring that, for example, a person enjoys freedom of speech. Rather, it was the case that there were no laws depriving a person of free speech. This situation contrasts sharply with many other democracies, where those rights are set out explicitly on paper and are usually an integral part of a codified constitution. In the United States, for example, the Bill of Rights forms the first ten amendments to the Constitution.

This position was criticised by many human rights organisations, which regarded the lack of an entrenched set of rights in the UK as an invitation to over-mighty governments to chip away at the liberties that citizens had enjoyed, effectively by default. Britain did sign the European Convention on Human Rights in 1950, but successive British governments have fallen foul of it on many occasions since then.

New Labour and the Human Rights Act

The Labour Party in its 1997 general election manifesto promised to incorporate the European Convention on Human Rights, and this duly came into force in October 2000. For the first time, a wide-ranging law was introduced, stating the rights of citizens in the United Kingdom. The following is a summary of the areas covered by the main articles of the Human Rights Act 1998:

- Article 2: the right to life
- Article 3: freedom from torture or inhuman or degrading treatment or punishment
- Article 4: freedom from slavery or forced labour
- Article 5: personal freedom
- Article 6: the right to a fair trial
- Article 7: no punishment without law
- Article 8: the protection of private and family life
- Article 9: freedom of thought, conscience and religion
- Article 10: freedom of expression
- Article 11: freedom of assembly and association
- Article 12: the right to marry
- Article 14: freedom from discrimination

In addition, the Human Rights Act 1998 has a number of protocols relating to certain other rights:

- Protocol 1, Article 1: protection of property

- Protocol 1, Article 2: the right to education
- Protocol 1, Article 3: the right to free elections
- Protocol 6: abolition of the death penalty

The Human Rights Act is not entrenched, however, and is subject to amendment. The British government has already made changes to the Act with regard to the treatment of terrorists. Only after many years on the statute book will the Act begin to resemble a revered part of the UK constitution, and given the changes referred to above, the signs may not be promising.

The judiciary and the protection of rights

Judicial review

Clearly one important way in which judges can protect rights is by the application of the Human Rights Act. A citizen may go to court if he or she feels that the government or any other public body (such as a devolved assembly) has acted in contravention of the Act. The court can, in most instances, overrule the body if it agrees with the complaint; the exception is Parliament, whose acts may be judged incompatible, but cannot be set aside or amended by a judge.

Other examples of judicial review are where citizens believe that a minister, for example, has acted beyond the powers granted to him or in law (*ultra vires*). If a government department acts beyond these powers, the actions may be struck down in the courts. Consequently, Acts of Parliament may be effectively upheld against abuse by politicians and public bodies.

Judicial review may be applied for by an individual or an organisation. A judge is asked to decide on the legality of a particular executive action. The judge can reject the application, in which case the actions of the government are not curtailed, or consider the application valid and require the government or public body to stop what it is doing pending a full hearing of the matter in court.

Michael Heseltine was declared to have acted *ultra vires* in 1992 when he announced a major pit closure programme. The programme had to be halted pending proper consultation (although in the end it went through). More significant were the number of times that Conservative home secretary Michael Howard was deemed to have acted *ultra vires* over prison sentencing. More recently, the Blair government was challenged by the Law Lords about the detention without trial of terrorism suspects, and this led to the government having to change the law.

A recurring theme in the study of modern British politics is the extent to which the executive has become over-dominant in comparison to, say, the legislature. The courts can provide a check on the actions of governments and in this way provide Parliament with the safeguard that its legislation is not being perverted by ministers and other public servants.

If a citizen is deemed to have had natural justice denied to him or her, a judge may intervene. This happened in the case of the directors of the engineering company Matrix-Churchill, who were to stand trial for illegally exporting parts for a supergun to Iraq. Their defence was that the Department of Trade and Industry knew about the sales. Before the trial, government ministers signed 'public interest immunity' certificates which effectively prevented the details of this defence being used as evidence. The judge ruled that the trial should not go ahead, since without this key information, the men would be denied natural justice.

Other ways to redress grievances

There are a number of other mechanisms for the protection of rights, which can be summarised as follows:

Tribunals

These exist in a variety of guises. Workers can go to an industrial tribunal to bring cases of unfair dismissal. Disputes over tax may be settled at Inland Revenue tribunals. There are also tribunals to deal with disputes involving social security.

Ombudsmen

Parliament, local government and the National Health Service all have commissioners to deal with cases where citizens feel they have been treated unfairly or been the subject of maladministration.

Europe

Citizens can apply to the European Court of Justice where they feel that their rights are protected by European law. The usual areas of complaint are in employment law and consumer law, and regulations concerning benefit payments.

Problems in protecting rights

As mentioned above, the Human Rights Act is not entrenched and therefore future governments can make changes to it or even repeal it altogether. Additionally, judges cannot apply the Act against Parliament, although they can give a ruling of incompatibility.

Some government legislation has eroded the rights of certain groups of citizens. In the 1980s, a series of Acts concerned with industrial relations and employment restricted the rights and activities of organised labour unions. Apart from the adoption of the Social Chapter of the Treaty of Maastricht, the Blair government has not restored any of these rights.

The laws on official secrecy were tightened in the late 1980s as a result of the Clive Ponting trial, where Ponting successfully argued that his action in leaking documents to an MP about the sinking of an Argentine battle cruiser in the Falklands war was justified on the basis of the national interest. The new legislation offers no public interest clause.

Over the past 20 years both Labour and Conservative governments have introduced legislation to increase police powers to stop and search suspects and to deal with public order violations with more vigour.

After the terrorist attacks in New York in September 2001 and in London in July 2005, the government has sought to increase the time that terrorist suspects can be held without charge. It failed in its bid to have the maximum time raised to 90 days in late 2005. In 2008 it wanted to have the time raised from 28 days to 42, arguing that the police need sufficient time to investigate terrorist crimes. Many critics from groups such as Liberty condemn such detention as major infringements on the rights of citizens, claiming that there is no evidence such time is needed.

Relations with the European Union

The courts in the UK are subject to European law, where applicable. Existing Acts may be set aside or amended if they go against European law, and new legislation must be drafted so that it does not come into conflict with European law. The UK courts must accept and enforce decisions of the European Court of Justice.

The EU has eroded sovereignty in a number of respects. The UK Parliament became subject to the primacy of European law on ratifying the Treaty of Rome in 1972. The UK could be taken to the European Court of Justice if it was seen to be in contravention of European law, for example in the *Factortame* case. The UK courts may have inferior status in some circumstances.

The European Convention on Human Rights is a non-EU agreement, effectively incorporated into the Human Rights Act of 1998. Judges have made frequent reference to the convention when giving their judgements. In June 2006, the High Court quashed six 'control orders' which allowed terror suspects to be held without charge. The judge, Mr Justice Sullivan, cited Article 5 of the European Convention on Human Rights, which outlaws indefinite detention without trial. He declared that control orders were incompatible with this article of the convention.

Judicial independence and neutrality

Tip

This part of the topic is often the cause of considerable confusion for candidates sitting the Unit 2 examination. The main problem is that insufficient distinction is made between the two concepts. Indeed, many students believe that the two are one and the same. While it is true that the concepts are linked, they remain quite distinct and, given the narrowness of the specification in this particular topic, there is a good chance that either or both will come up in the examination.

Judicial independence

In the UK several features protect judicial independence from the other parts of the UK political system. They may be summarised as follows:

Security of tenure

Judges have security of tenure; in other words, they cannot be easily sacked from their jobs. (Of course, they can be dismissed for improper behaviour.) The idea is that judges do not have to worry about their personal positions when deliberating upon legal matters. Furthermore, the salaries of judges are not determined by politicians, but by the same independent salary review process that determines the levels of remuneration for senior civil servants.

The 2005 Constitutional Reform Act included a guarantee of continued judicial independence. It established a Judicial Appointments Commission, with the appointment of judges on merit, via advertised vacancies and interviews. This move dramatically reduced the role of the government in the judicial appointments process.

In addition the legislation provides for the creation of a United Kingdom Supreme Court, to replace the House of Lords as the highest court in the land from October 2009. After this time cases will no longer be heard by the House of Lords, removing one of the overlaps in the UK constitution, to create a separation between the House of Lords' role as a legislature and its role as a court.

Legal immunity

Judges have legal immunity from civil actions in their capacity as judges. They are effectively protected by the law in respect of the proceedings that go on in their courts; this is important because otherwise a judge might be prevented from directing the course of a trial to ensure that justice is done.

Sub judice rule

Sub judice is the rule that prevents public mention of most matters under consideration in the courts (to prevent undue political pressure). However, court hearings are open to the public and press (see below), and judges must give full reasons for their decisions. Once again, this limits the scope for political interference in the process of justice.

Media interest

Except in cases where the judge has imposed reporting restrictions on journalists, the media can gain access to the courts. This is especially important for cases involving questions of civil liberties. In such cases, widespread publicity effectively prevents the politicians from interfering with judges' decisions.

Support from Parliament

There is a parliamentary convention that judges are not criticised in Parliament. This is important in protecting judges from political interference. In addition, this convention prevents politicians from being manoeuvred into the judicial arena by the media or pressure groups.

Limitations on judicial independence

The convention of judicial independence needs to be placed in a contemporary context-ual framework. There are a number of concerns about the extent to which judges are truly independent of the other agents of the UK constitution.

Even after the changes of the 2005 Constitutional Reform Act, the executive will maintain a residual role in the appointment of judges. These will be, in the main, senior members of the judiciary. It may be argued that there remains potential for political interference in the careers of judges and that this calls into question the extent to which judges are politically independent. Clearly the new Judicial Appointments Commission is a welcome move, but the question remains as to who will choose the members of this selection body.

As discussed in the section on constitutions (pages 12–13), the UK political system is not characterised by a rigid separation between the executive, legislature and judiciary. The head of the judiciary, the Lord Chancellor, is also a member of the cabinet. The present incumbent, Jack Straw, holds the position in residual form, with his main responsibilities being as head of the Ministry of Justice. At one time the Lord Chancellor was the very personification of the lack of separation of powers, being in charge of the judiciary, a member of the cabinet and the speaker of the House of Lords.

The Law Lords (who comprise the UK's highest court) are also members of the House of Lords. This further overlap of powers makes it difficult to argue that there is true independence for members of the judiciary, not only because of the impact that their proximity to the political system might have on them, but also because of the impact that they, as unelected individuals, might have upon the democratic system.

Although the judiciary is, in theory, free from political interference, increased media interest in judicial matters has led to a number of areas for concern. While it is proper in a democracy that the media ensure that public opinion is taken into account when judges are deliberating on specific cases, there is a worry that this is perhaps going too far in some cases.

There have been a number of high-profile cases where the press has criticised sentences given out by judges, and pressure has been put on the government to act on such matters. Many newspapers criticised the sentence given to Maxine Carr for her part in the Soham murder case. Perhaps more worryingly, there have been occasions when politicians have felt compelled to become involved, as did the home secretary, Michael Howard, when he tried to interfere with the sentences given to the killers of James Bulger.

Judicial neutrality

Judicial independence and judicial neutrality are linked, but they are not the same thing. Whereas independence refers to the relationship between judges and other parts of the constitution, neutrality is concerned with the issue of political bias and personal prejudices. These are often associated with the social background, education and lifestyle of the individuals who hold judicial office.

The theory of judicial neutrality is that regardless of their own background, beliefs or party political inclinations, judges must act in a way that does not exhibit bias. This could be in dealing with a defendant in a court case or in the way that the government is treated when considering a judicial review, for example. Justice ought to be blind to all factors that are not of relevance to the case in question. In theory, everyone should be equal in the eyes of the courts and it is the duty of the judge to apply such equality.

Limitations on judicial neutrality

There have been a number of reasons in recent years to question whether the theory of judicial neutrality is working in practice. One of the main critics of the political role of the judiciary is J. A. G. Griffiths, who argues that judges display a striking similarity, being in the main male, white, upper middle class, and public-school educated with degrees from the universities of Oxford or Cambridge. It has also been suggested that judges discriminate against women, racial minorities, and any other group that is poorly represented in the judiciary itself.

This view essentially argues that judges cannot be neutral because of their own backgrounds. It is clear that Griffiths believes that most judges exhibit a conservative bias. In this view, judges are seen as defenders of the status quo — the existing political and social order.

Griffiths argues that judges base their view of what is in the public interest on three factors: first, the interests of the state; second, the preservation of law and order; and third, the judges' views on social and political issues of the day.

Despite the existence of a supposed 'new breed' of judges, as late as 1993 over 95% of judges were men, there was only one woman judge at High Court level or above, and there were no non-white judges at that level. Less than 1% of solicitors are non-white and over three-quarters are men. Over four-fifths of barristers are male, and it is from barristers that most judges will be recruited for the foreseeable future.

If there is any conflict between fundamental rights of the individual and the interests of the state, it is argued that judges will usually side with the latter. Freedom of expression is often a casualty when the national interest is invoked. In the late 1980s, the government attempted to suppress the memoirs of Peter Wright, a former operative of the security service MI5. Judges sided with the government in arguing that the publication of his book *Spycatcher*, or extracts from it, would compromise national security, and they effectively banned newspapers from even mentioning its name in print. It could be argued that the restrictions on newspaper coverage of the debate about the publication of the book were a gross restriction on the rights of a free press and of freedom of expression.

There is considerable scope for judicial bias as to what constitutes the national interest. The case of Clive Ponting in the mid-1980s testifies to this. After the Falklands

War in 1982, confidential material was leaked to a Labour MP, indicating that the Thatcher government had provided inaccurate information regarding the sinking of the Argentine cruiser the *General Belgrano*. This leak was highly embarrassing to the government, and a senior civil servant in the Ministry of Defence, Clive Ponting, came forward to admit making the disclosure. He was tried for offences against the Official Secrets Act. During his trial, Ponting used the national interest clause in the Act to justify his actions. The judge advised the jury that it was for the government and not for an individual to determine what was in the national interest. His view was that Ponting had no justification for his actions. Fortunately for Ponting, the jury did not agree with this analysis and found him not guilty.

The preservation of an ordered society, Griffiths has argued, is a very important consideration for judges when they hear cases in court. Judges have been particularly harsh in dealing with crimes that appear to challenge the very fabric of the state. The handling of a series of cases involving alleged terrorists would return to haunt the UK judicial system years later. Years after the release of the 'Birmingham Six' and the 'Guildford Four', people whose original convictions for terrorist offences were overturned, it is worth remarking how willing the judges were at the time of those trials to dismiss objections to the way interviews were conducted and statements were collected by the police. This evidence was shown years later to have been largely fabricated. The preservation of order, or at least the appearance of the preservation of order, seemed to have outweighed any consideration of fairness to the defendants.

Robert Kee, in his book *Trial & Error* about the Guildford Four, claims that Mr Justice Donaldson, the trial judge, summed up impeccably (but unfairly) in favour of the prosecution.

If Griffiths is to be believed, groups whose aims are at variance with the beliefs and attitudes of the judiciary and who protest in ways which result in a certain amount of lawlessness are unlikely to find judges being tolerant with them for the sake of the liberties of free speech or free assembly.

One of the main planks of what became known as Thatcherism was the determination of the government in the 1980s to rein in the power of the trade unions by introducing legislation that made a number of union practices illegal. As a consequence, the courts became involved in a number of industrial disputes during this time. The attitude of the courts, even towards those demonstrations and pickets that did not result in violence, was to seek to curtail union activity. During the 1984–85 miners' strike, judges appeared eager to punish any striking miner whose protests went beyond the legitimate. Union leaders such as Arthur Scargill argued that the judges were simply doing the dirty work of the Thatcher government, and that the so-called impartial court system was rendered unjust by the clear anti-union bias of the judiciary.

This view is given credence by the number of civil cases where judges sided with employers by ordering the sequestration (confiscation) of union funds in disputes such as the miners' strike and the print unions' conflict with newspaper bosses including Eddie Shah and Rupert Murdoch.

Government legislation in the 1980s was directed towards strengthening the position of employers and weakening employees. Inevitably, because that is their function and their role whether they like it or not, the courts were drawn into the conflict and required to make legal decisions that were also political. The courts regard an industrial dispute as essentially one where the 'enjoyment of private property' is being interfered with. It is on this basis that they are so ready to grant interim injunctions, the effect of which is greatly to diminish the workers' bargaining power by suspending the right to strike.

Contemporary debates on judicial neutrality

The Griffiths thesis on judicial neutrality is well established, and left-wing politicians have made similar points for several decades. To some extent this is a problem for students of contemporary politics. In recent years there has been a growing body of evidence that the nature of the judiciary is changing and that the traditional views about judges being conservative are now, in fact, out of date.

In the early 1990s, it became clear that more and more judges were willing to stand up to the Conservative government. Indeed, it appeared that a new generation of judges was arriving on the bench and that these judges did not conform to the stereotypical picture painted by Griffiths.

Judges argued in favour of the unions and against the employers in the 1989 dock strike over the abolition of the National Dock Labour scheme. In 1985, the health and social security secretary, Norman Fowler, was defeated in a number of court cases in both the High Court and the Court of Appeal as the judges outlawed his new rules on social security benefits because of a lack of consultation by the department.

Judges such as Lord Justice Taylor and Lords Bingham, Browne Wilkinson and Hoffman were rising to high positions in the hierarchy of the judiciary. These judges were not conservative, anti-liberal defenders of the status quo; rather they appeared to be willing to challenge the government and favour the incremental absorption of the European Convention on Human Rights into English law on a case-by-case basis.

David Rose, in his article 'Silent revolution' in the *Observer* newspaper (9 May 1993), discussed this new breed of judges and some of the cases that indicate they may no longer be stereotyped as conservative defenders of the status quo. Indeed, the number of cases where judges have found against Conservative home secretaries, such as Kenneth Baker and Michael Howard, easily match the opposition that Labour home secretaries Jack Straw and David Blunkett faced from the judges' bench.

Of course, this only demonstrates that the nature of judicial bias is changing, not that it is disappearing. At one time commentators could claim a conservative bias among judges, but if Rose is to be believed it would appear that there is now a greater bias towards a liberal interpretation of the law. The question mark about whether judges can remain politically neutral remains.

Questions
&
Answers

This section of the guide provides you with four questions on Unit 2: Governing the UK covering each of the main topics on the specification. They are in the style of the Edexcel unit test, which has four questions, two of which are divided into three parts and two of which are essay-type questions.

Guidance notes after each question outline how to answer the question and how to avoid any pitfalls. These notes are followed by A- and C-grade responses.

Examiner's comments

The answers are interspersed with examiner's comments, preceded by the icon **e**. These comments identify why marks have been given and where improvements might be made, especially in the C-grade answers.

The executive

Study the source below and answer the questions (a) to (c) that follow.

The cabinet and the prime minister

The cabinet consists of only the most senior ministers in the government. Normally each government department has as its most senior minister a secretary of state who is a member of the cabinet — the secretary of state for health, for example, or the home secretary (whose proper title is the secretary of state for home affairs). Not all members of the cabinet are heads of government departments; some cabinet ministers have other, non-departmental responsibilities. They include the government chief whip and the leader of the House of Commons, as well as so-called ministers without portfolio, who may have some important party function.

The cabinet is the place where collective decision-making takes place and it is crucial that, once a policy stance has been agreed by ministers in the cabinet, the government as a whole stands in full agreement with this policy. In this sense the cabinet, and the government more widely, must be seen to show unity.

The cabinet now meets only once a week and for less than an hour. It is difficult to conceive that a body which meets for so little time can really have a grip on the political system. In reality, the cabinet acts as a final nod to policy and often simply endorses the recommendations of other forums, such as cabinet sub-committees.

In the past, at least, the cabinet was seen to be the central part of the British political system. More recently, however, a number of commentators have questioned the importance of the cabinet in the decision-making process. One of the reasons for this is the rise in power of the prime minister, which has left unanswered the questions as to what the cabinet actually does and how powerful and important it is.

(a) Using the source, describe the main features of the British cabinet. (5 marks)

(b) Describe the powers of the prime minister. (10 marks)

(c) What are the limits on the powers of the prime minister? (25 marks)

Total: 40 marks

(a) In the part (a) stimulus-based question, you are being asked to use the source material, not to copy it out. To achieve full marks, you need to summarise what you see in the source and put it into your own words. These questions often require a brief description of a political institution. Candidates should be well prepared for questions such as these; however, although they are worth only a few marks, they can prove quite troublesome. This question is asking for a brief description of the features, rather then the functions of the cabinet. The important point to understand is that it is impossible to say everything about an institution in a short response, but more than just a single point has to be made. The aim is to give the flavour of the institution in about 100 words.

(b) Three well-explained points would normally be sufficient for a part (b) response such as this. Indeed, in a number of such questions, a numerical requirement is specified in the wording of the question. If the question does not specify a number and if there is time in which to make extra points, it does no harm to include as many explained points as possible. If time is a restricting factor and you have to choose between writing three well-explained points and making four or five points, less fully explained, the best advice would be to go for fewer, better-explained points. Answers containing many points and no explanation are likely to fall into the C-grade range of marks.

(c) A response offering no illustrative material probably cannot achieve high marks for this type of question. It simply asks for the limitations on the power of the prime minister and does not require counter-arguments, so any candidates who answer the question as if it asks them to 'assess the power of the prime minister' will be wasting up to half of their time on irrelevant material.

■ ■ ■

A-grade answer

(a) The cabinet is the body that contains the most senior government ministers. These are normally the heads of government departments and other non-departmental ministers such as the chief whip. The cabinet is where collective government takes place. All decisions reached in cabinet must be defended publicly by members of the government to demonstrate that the government is united over policy. The cabinet meets briefly only once a week, which means that it cannot deal with policy matters in great detail. Rather it is a place where final approval is given to government policy. It has been argued that the power of the cabinet has declined in recent decades as the prime minister has come to dominate the political scene.

This response offers a number of features of the cabinet, using the source material. The key skill here is to distill the essential elements from the passage of text. Candidates who get bogged down in detail find they spend too long on the question, leaving insufficient time for the remaining parts. It is important to remember that this question is worth just 5 marks, which means that it should be allocated just 5 marks' worth of time (about 5 minutes)

(b) The prime minister is the head of government. He or she is the most senior minister in the cabinet and the political representative of the state at international gatherings. When the UK chaired the G8 and held the EU presidency, it was the prime minister who chaired these important meetings on behalf of the UK.

Another important power of the prime minister is that of ministerial appointment. This includes promotions, demotions and dismissals. On taking over as prime minister at the end of June 2007, Gordon Brown formed a new cabinet, appointing Jacqui Smith as home secretary and promoting Alistair Darling to the post of chancellor of the exchequer. The prime minister also makes a number of non-ministerial appointments, for example the chair of the BBC. Finally, the prime minister makes recommendations about new members of the House of Lords. Just prior to the 2005 general election, Tony Blair elevated sufficient Labour supporters to make the party the largest single party in the upper chamber.

Many prime ministerial powers derive from the royal prerogative, i.e. those powers traditionally in the hands of the monarch. Officially, the monarch dissolves Parliament before a general election. In reality, the timing is all down to when the prime minister makes the request. Another prerogative power is the declaration of war, which although it is done in the monarch's name, is a decision taken after cabinet consultation by the prime minister.

Another function of the prime minister is to lead the majority party in the House of Commons. Gordon Brown took over as the leader of the Labour Party and it was by this route that he came to be asked to become the prime minister. These two roles essentially go hand in hand. When Margaret Thatcher resigned from leadership of the Conservative Party in 1990, she had to resign as prime minister as well.

> ✏ Four substantial points are outlined above. This does not mean that it will always be necessary to be this thorough to secure an A grade. Quality is more important than the quantity — but there has to be some quantity. These points are all well explained, and the answer would receive 9 marks.

(c) The prime minister faces a number of constraints. He or she does not have total freedom when it comes to ministerial appointments. Loyal party colleagues will expect some reward in government. This may be particularly important during times of political difficulty for the government. Michael Heseltine was promoted to deputy prime minister as a reward for supporting John Major during a difficult time in 1995. The expectations of powerful colleagues may also limit the power of the prime minister's freedom to appoint ministers. Some individuals not only expect to be in the government but they may also expect a particular job. In 2005, there was little doubt that, on winning the general election, Tony Blair would keep Gordon Brown as chancellor of the exchequer, given the relative popularity of each man within the Labour Party at that time. The prime minister may also take notice of gender and ethnic factors. By the time of the 2005 general election, the Blair cabinet included five women and Paul Boateng, a black MP. Gordon Brown has appointed the country's first woman home secretary.

The prime minister may wish to have a balance of opinions and backgrounds within the party in the government. Clare Short did not subscribe to the 'New Labour' project, but she was included in Tony Blair's cabinet in 1997. John Prescott came from a totally different background from most of the rest of the Blair cabinet. Gordon Brown had the difficult task of ensuring former Blair loyalists were represented in his cabinet. John Hutton was one such high-profile appointment.

One of the key prerogative powers, the declaration of war, appears to be slipping from the prime minister's hands. In 2003, Tony Blair felt he had to go the House of Commons to seek approval for the Iraq war. During the 2005 general election campaign, Gordon Brown stated that future wars should be subject to similar parliamentary approval, perhaps limiting once and for all this once important power.

Leading a political party can also be a constraint on power; ultimately it can cost a prime minister his/her job, as Margaret Thatcher found in 1990. John Major similarly had difficulties with members of the Parliamentary Conservative Party, which undermined his authority with voters. Tony Blair faced similar problems following the 2005 general election and was ultimately forced to provide a timetable for his own departure. Many members of the Labour Party are unhappy about the leadership of Gordon Brown, with many calling for him to stand down. A prime minister who lacks party support may well also encounter greater resistance from senior cabinet colleagues. Tony Blair is said to have been in this position after the 2005 election. Cabinet ministers appear to be jockeying to succeed Gordon Brown should he decide to resign sooner rather than later.

The size of the government's majority in the House of Commons can affect the power of the prime minister. John Major led a government with a substantially reduced majority after the 1992 general election. His government struggled with a number of pieces of legislation thereafter (such as the ratification of the Maastricht Treaty in 1992–93). After the 2005 general election, the Blair government had a substantially reduced parliamentary majority and faced defeats on issues such as the detention of suspected terrorists. The same issue is threatening Gordon Brown, along with that of the abolition of the ten pence tax band.

The relations enjoyed between the prime minister and the media can affect the power of the prime minister. John Major's personal authority evaporated virtually overnight following the ERM crisis in 1992. Many previously sympathetic sections of the press turned on him and from then on he found greater difficulty leading his party and his government. Tony Blair, who had widespread media popularity in the mid-1990s, saw his media image decline substantially. After a promising first couple of months in power, Gordon Brown now has a very poor media image. Again, this affects the authority that the prime minister has within his party and in the country.

    ℓ This response covers the main demands of the question very well. A number of key issues are addressed, and they are illustrated with the use of contemporary examples. It would gain 23–24 marks.

■ ■ ■

C-grade answer

(a) The cabinet is another word for the top ministers. They meet at 10 Downing Street and discuss the major issues of the day. The prime minister sits at the head of the cabinet and chairs discussions at cabinet meetings. The cabinet makes important decisions which affect the policies that the government will follow. The prime minister appoints all cabinet ministers.

> This is a limited response. Its main focus is on the cabinet making important decisions, and there is insufficient reference to the source as a trigger for the key features. Indeed, there seems to be little reference at all to the stimulus material. It would achieve no more than 2 or 3 marks out of the 5 available.

(b) The prime minister has a number of functions. Perhaps the most important function is the power of appointment. One of the first tasks of any newly elected or re-elected prime minister is to appoint other members of the cabinet. There are many factors that the prime minister has to take into account when making such appointments, such as the age and experience as well as the expectations of his senior party colleagues. Gordon Brown, for example, was the obvious choice to put into the Treasury after the 1997 general election.

Another power is to call a general election. This is a significant power because it gives the prime minister the edge over other politicians, as he or she can call the election at a time convenient to his or her political party.

A final function of the prime minister is to declare war. This was seen clearly when Tony Blair sent British troops to fight with the Americans in Iraq in 2003.

> The problem with the first point made here is that too much of it is not relevant to the question asked. The first three sentences are fine: they state an important function and rate it as important. The remainder of the first paragraph, however, relates to a factor limiting the prime minister's power, and this is not needed to answer the question properly. The example given is only relevant to this, and so it is of only indirect relevance to the answer as a whole. The candidate could have spent the time more fruitfully examining the prime minister's other powers of appointment.
>
> Overall, this is a limited response, primarily because the points made are general, containing little in the way of specific explanation and offering few examples. One major concern is that there are no contemporary examples given; the latest prime minister mentioned in this response is Tony Blair. The final point about the declaration of war lacks the understanding and sophistication necessary for the example used — the Iraq war was the first time that Parliament had been consulted for its approval beforehand. This demonstrates that there are times when a poor choice of examples can damage your analysis. This response would achieve around 4 out of the 10 marks available.

(c) The prime minister is limited in the way he makes appointments. The prime minister needs to ensure that there is a left–right balance within the cabinet. Tony Blair had both wings included in government, including the likes of John Prescott on the left and Jack Straw on the right. Party loyalty is another important factor which limits the prime minister. After an election the prime minister is expected to reward colleagues who have shown personal loyalty. David Blunkett was a very loyal colleague of Tony Blair and he has recently been recalled to the cabinet. John Prescott remains as deputy prime minister because of his continued loyalty. Gordon Brown has attempted to keep Blairites in his cabinet.

Individual politicians may also expect to be appointed due to their seniority and experience. Gordon Brown has been a very effective chancellor of the exchequer, popular within his party, and the pressure was on for Tony Blair to keep him in this very important position after the 2005 general election. In this respect, any desire on the part of the prime minister for a more substantial cabinet reshuffle was limited. David Miliband must have expected a good job from Gordon Brown.

There are other factors that limit the prime minister's powers of appointment. Appointing more women to government is seen as providing a signal to other occupational fields. Similarly, the desire to include greater ethnic diversity at the top of British politics might be seen as a further constraint. Certainly the evidence of the Blair government since 1997 seems to bear this out.

✏ This response shows either a misreading of the question or an insufficiently wide grasp of the subject matter. It deals with only one of the powers of the prime minister — the power of appointment. Furthermore, the response examines only one aspect of appointment, that of ministers. In fact, the candidate deals with the topic very well, drawing upon examples to illustrate a number of well-made points. If the response had covered just one more power of the prime minister in similar depth, there would have been sufficient coverage to access a higher range of marks. However, this response is too narrow to get more than 10 or 11 marks.

Parliament

Study the source below and answer the questions (a) to (c) that follow.

Reforms of Parliament since 1997

The Blair government has made a number of reforms to both the House of Commons and the House of Lords. After the general election of 1997, it changed the way Prime Minister's Question Time was organised to a single half-hour slot every week. In recognition of the large increase in the number of women MPs, the government also moved to end all-night sittings in a bid to introduce more family-friendly working hours for MPs. The prime minister has also opened himself up to greater parliamentary scrutiny by appearing before the House of Commons Liaison Committee twice a year.

Shortly after becoming prime minister, Gordon Brown suggested that he wanted to strengthen Parliament by transferring some of the prerogative powers that his predecessors had enjoyed, including the power to declare war.

Perhaps the most controversial reforms have taken place in the House of Lords. The Labour Party has long been against the unelected upper chamber and keen to put an end to the hereditary principle. The government moved to end the right to sit in the Lords for all but 92 hereditary peers. This means that the overwhelming majority of members of the Lords are now nominated.

In 2007, the government published proposals to complete the process of Lords reform by abolishing the remaining hereditary peers. The majority of members of the House of Commons favour a fully elected second chamber. The Lords themselves voted in preference for an all-appointed second chamber. Gordon Brown has renewed his commitment to reforming the second chamber.

(a) **Using the source material, what have been the main reforms of Parliament since 1997?** (5 marks)

(b) **What are the main criticisms of the reforms of Parliament since 1997?** (10 marks)

(c) **What are the main arguments for and against an elected second chamber?** (25 marks)

Total: 40 marks

(a) This question requires you to comment upon the reforms in your own words. Use of the source material is clearly important here, but simply copying out whole sections will not earn you top marks. You need to identify the main reforms and put them together in a paragraph.

(b) As with part (c) of the previous question, your use of time is critical here. You will have 10 minutes to write your response, within which time you are expected to offer a range of fully supported points. This question requires a one-sided analysis; you will receive no credit for writing about the benefits of parliamentary reform.

(c) This question asks for a balanced view, so it is important that you analyse both sides of the argument in your response. To obtain the highest marks, you are expected to explain a number of relevant points using examples. You should be familiar with the key arguments in the debate about turning the House of Lords into a second chamber. This question differs from that in part (b), which requires you to examine only one side of a debate.

■ ■ ■

A-grade answer

(a) There have been changes to both houses of Parliament. The changes made to the House of Commons have been, in the main, procedural, such as making the sitting hours more family-friendly after the big influx of women MPs. Other changes have involved the way the prime minister is scrutinised, including changing Prime Minister's Question Time to one slot per week and the PM's appearances before the House of Commons Liaison Committee every 6 months. The changes to the House of Lords have been more structural, and the source points out that these have been more controversial. The Labour Party had always opposed the hereditary principle and the Blair government passed legislation to allow only 92 hereditary peers to sit in the House of Lords. Gordon Brown has announced some transfer of prerogative powers to Parliament.

This answer contains the information in the source, but it has been paraphrased rather than simply copied out. The candidate shows evidence of contextual understanding by introducing reforms to the House of Commons as procedural, and describing those to the House of Lords as structural. This is not essential, but it conveys to the examiner that the candidate is dealing with the information in a polished manner. This is a confident answer and would be recognised as such by the examiner, receiving the maximum 5 marks.

(b) The reforms of Parliament so far can be criticised from two perspectives. First, there is the view that they have gone too far. Second, there is the view that the reforms have not gone far enough (a criticism usually coming from groups such as Charter 88).

Many of those in favour of more radical reform argue that the government has acted too slowly. Most criticism concerns the second chamber, but many Liberal Democrats argue that there has been little meaningful reform of the Commons, particularly as regards changing the way it is elected. The Blair government failed to deliver on its promise of a referendum on this issue, and it is argued that the Commons will remain an undemocratic chamber.

Despite Labour's promises before the 1997 general election, it took 2 years before any action was taken over the second chamber, and when it was, most of the people left in it had been appointed on the nod of the prime minister. Indeed, Tony Blair chose Lord Wakeham to chair a committee to investigate the future of the House of Lords. His report was seen by many on the left as being insufficiently radical. Eleven years on from the election of the new Labour government, there are little more than intentions about the future reform.

Some critics claim that the reforms have gone too far. Traditionalists in the House of Commons have decried the changes to the sitting hours of the chamber, complaining that those MPs who could not commute home each evening would better spend their time debating in the Commons than sitting in their London flats.

Others argue that the changes to Prime Minister's Question Time have reduced the occasions when the prime minister can be scrutinised by the whole House of Commons. As such, there has been an erosion of some of the government's accountability to Parliament.

The Conservatives, long seen as the party of caution when it comes to matters involving constitutional reform, have been critical of the changes that have been made to the House of Lords so far. They now call for a fully elected second chamber.

✍ This is a full response that addresses the question directly. The main criticisms of parliamentary reform since 1997 are explained well. In addition, the response looks at the criticisms from two distinct perspectives and would be given 9 marks.

You could be awarded a grade A without making all the above points, but the more points that you make, the more insight the examiner has into the breadth of your knowledge and understanding. In the case of this question, it is perhaps most important to offer the analysis from the dual perspective outlined above.

(c) Clearly an elected second chamber would be more democratic. Currently the House of Lords is a largely appointed chamber, with a rump of 92 hereditary peers. If members of the second chamber were elected then the people would be expressing their will over the whole of Parliament and not only over one of its chambers, as is the situation now.

Those who hold power should be periodically answerable for their decisions and actions. An elected second chamber would be answerable, and as such there would be greater political accountability to the voters through the ballot box. At present, no lord has a constituency, so ultimately none of them are in any way accountable.

Linked to this point, a fully elected second chamber would lend the political process added legitimacy. Currently only the Commons can claim such legitimacy and as such the Lords is under pressure to give way when confronted by the more legitimate chamber. If both chambers were elected, it would be clear that

AS Government & Politics

legislation had the consent of the people. It may be argued that such legislation would be based on the prerogative of inter-chamber cooperation based on shared legitimacy.

Overall, an elected second chamber would provide the UK with a more modern Parliament to make it effective in the twenty-first century. The country would lose an anachronistic part of the constitution with the replacement of a non-elected Parliament. It could be argued that, at the moment, institutions such as the House of Lords make Britain appear to commentators abroad as if it is obsessed by tradition and history.

One of the strongest arguments against an elected second chamber is that there would be potential for gridlock between the first and second elected chambers if there were a disagreement to be resolved. If the second chamber were elected using a proportional voting system, its members could even claim to have greater legitimacy than the first chamber, which is elected using the simple plurality system.

There might be a question over the calibre of those wanting to serve in an elected second chamber. Lord Wakeham talked about it being the 'fourth eleven' — in other words, the team for the weakest players. This would be a particular problem if the powers of the second chamber were limited.

There would be the loss of some talented and gifted individuals who have excelled in their own particular fields — the arts, sciences, business and industry — as well as in politics, and are at the moment appointed as life peers. In their place would be individuals who might see membership of the second chamber as just a stepping-stone to the House of Commons, rather than a place worthy in itself.

Allied to the above point is the fact that, currently, the House of Lords has some skilled and well-respected groups working within it. For example, the House of Lords European Committee has a very high reputation among European Union officials working in Brussels.

While it would be hard to argue for a return to the hereditary dominance of the House of Lords, the present structure of the second chamber is probably just right; most of the hereditary element has now disappeared, and this could be regarded as a significant advance. Much of the rest of the Lords does a valuable job that might not be done as well by simply electing replacements.

🖉 This is a full response that addresses the question directly. The main arguments both for and against an elected second chamber are explained well. In addition, where appropriate a number of illustrations add weight to arguments being made. This response would receive 22–23 marks.

■ ■ ■

C-grade answer

(a) After the general election of 1997, the government changed the way Prime Minister's Question Time was organised to a single half-hour slot every week. In recognition of the large increase in the number of women MPs, the government also moved to end all-night sittings in a bid to introduce more family-friendly working hours for MPs. The prime minister has also opened himself up to greater parliamentary scrutiny by appearing before the House of Commons Liaison Committee twice a year.

> ⓔ This answer has simply been copied word for word from the source. While the examiner does not expect new information to be introduced in the response, and the source has everything required to get full marks, the question asks candidates to 'comment' and this does not mean copy.
>
> Another problem with the response is that it is limited to the reforms of the House of Commons. Perhaps the candidate spent the allotted 5 minutes copying out the first paragraph and felt the need to move on to the next part of the question. This response would achieve about 2 marks.

(b) Some of the main criticisms of the reforms of Parliament come from people who believe that they have gone too far and are doing untold damage to the constitution. These traditionalists argue that Parliament functions well as it is and that it should be left alone. Changes should only take place if there is a real need and it is clear that the reform will make things better. Parliament already has the power to make changes to itself if it feels it is necessary. Long-lasting and well-established practices have been lost with these changes to the upper chamber, for example. The Lords had been able to stand up for itself in the past to try to overcome elective dictatorship in the Commons.

The Conservatives are staunch defenders of Parliament and they see the reforms to the House of Lords from a negative standpoint. They are normally cautious on these sorts of issues and have been critical of the changes that have been made to the House of Lords so far. They have accused the government of leaving the Lords vulnerable to being filled with government sympathisers. They have been similarly critical of Blair's changes to Prime Minister's Question Time, saying that the opposition does not have as many opportunities to question the prime minister as it used to.

> ⓔ The main problem with this response is that it does not specifically address the question. Too many of the points are aimed at reform of the House of Lords, rather than the issue of parliamentary reform in general. What saved this answer from receiving a lower mark was the reference to Prime Minister's Question Time. However, when compared to the A-grade response, in which the candidate tailors all the points specifically to what is asked in the question, it is clear why this answer is likely to achieve only about 4 of the 10 marks on offer.

(c) The current House of Lords does a good job. Conservatives would question the need for reform. Furthermore, the House of Lords is part of our political traditions and as such should be protected from those who want change simply for the sake of change.

The House of Lords has a wealth of talent which would be lost if the current system was done away with. Many of the current members come from backgrounds where they have proved themselves with distinction. This is a powerful argument against reform.

One of the main reasons for not having an elected second chamber is that there would be a risk of political deadlock between it and the House of Commons if there were disagreements. At the moment, the government can use the Parliament Act to overcome the blocking tactics of the House of Lords.

It could be argued that the House of Lords has been reformed enough and that it should be reformed no further. The fact that Tony Blair was pulled in two directions, by those who wanted more reform and those who wanted to go back, probably means that he has got it about right with the current situation.

On the other hand, it must be argued that an elected second chamber would be more democratic, since it would literally give power to the people. This power would be to vote for members of the second chamber as well as the House of Commons in general elections.

This response lacks balance and it is not until the last paragraph that an argument in favour of electing the second chamber is introduced. This could be for a number of reasons. Perhaps the candidate did not read the question properly and it was only at the last minute that he or she realised that arguments in favour were needed. Perhaps the candidate did not have anything to say on the subject.

Too many of the points are aimed at reform of the House of Lords in general, rather than the issue of an elected second chamber in particular, although this is dealt with briefly in the third paragraph. Indeed, it could also be argued that the final paragraph implies the idea of election when speculating on future reform. However, in failing to tailor all the points specifically to what was asked in the question, this answer would achieve about 11 out of the 25 marks on offer. The response is brief and there is insufficient explanation of the points made. A further weakness is the lack of illustrations or examples.

Constitutions

Should the United Kingdom adopt a codified constitution?

This question carries 40 marks and candidates have about 40 minutes to answer it. It is therefore an essay question. Essays enable candidates to explore a topic and develop a series of arguments around a particular question. The examiner will expect both range and depth in the response. A single-side answer making a couple of points will be unlikely to secure a high mark.

This particular question expects a balanced response — arguments from both sides of the debate need to be deployed in order to access the full range of marks available.

■ ■ ■

A-grade answer

A codified constitution clearly indicates the nature of the distribution of political power within a state, identifying those persons and institutions responsible for particular actions and therefore assisting the process of political accountability. In the United States, for example, the president and the Congress each fulfil specific functions. Voters are able to express their views on the various players in US politics because the Constitution has set down these arrangements and they cannot be altered without a wide degree of political consensus. Voters are able to make the distinction about who or what they are voting for in different elections by 'splitting the ticket', which could involve voting for a Democratic presidential candidate while voting for a Republican who is running for a seat in the House of Representatives.

Another argument in favour of codified constitutions is that they can limit the power of the executive. In the UK, a government with a parliamentary majority can do almost anything it wants to do. The UK government faces few effective constraints, unlike the executive in the USA, which has its limits determined by a codified constitution. This can be argued as being more democratic. It may also be argued that the US-style statute of limitations, which restricts the president to two terms in office, is an effective means of curbing the power of individuals over the longer term.

A codified constitution that is difficult to amend protects citizens from governments changing fundamental laws just because it suits political expediency. A government that operates within the context of a codified constitution cannot reform the political structures for its own ends with ease. In this sense there are built-in safeguards in such a system. In the United States, only constitutional reforms that enjoy a high degree of political consensus have any chance of being implemented. This does offer some assurance that the Constitution cannot easily be changed for narrow party-political advantage.

This may be compared to the UK system, for example, which allows governments to alter political structures by use of a parliamentary majority. In the 1980s, the Thatcher government abolished a swathe of metropolitan local councils, including the Greater London Council, because in the eyes of some observers these councils were attempting to challenge the powers of central government. It may be argued that such changes could not happen in a country, such as the United States, which has a codified constitution.

A codified constitution can also be used to define and protect the rights of citizens. If the process of amendment is a rigorous one, then these rights will be difficult to alter. Changes to citizens' rights will not occur without widespread political and popular support. In the United States, the Bill of Rights is the part of the Constitution dealing with fundamental rights. It forms the first ten amendments to the Constitution. The rights of US citizens cannot easily be taken away.

Once again, this contrasts sharply to states that do not have codified constitutions. In the UK, rights have until recently been unspecified and expressed in negative terms — a right being something that the law so far does not prohibit. Many believe that the introduction of the Human Rights Act in the UK is an important step to UK citizens' rights being entrenched. Only a codified constitution can do this, however, as the Human Rights Act can easily be amended. Indeed, there have already been changes to the Act in response to the increased risk of terrorism. Critics argue that the relative ease with which such changes can be made renders a country without a codified constitution subject to rights abuse by its government.

The first point to be made against a codified constitution is its lack of flexibility compared to the uncodified UK constitution. In the USA, for example, the codified constitution requires quite a convoluted process of amendment. This means that the political system does not adapt quickly to changing circumstances and does not provide adequate responses to new situations. It has been claimed that, following the terrorist attacks in the United States on 11 September 2001, the UK government was able to respond much more quickly than the US administration by changing the scope of the Human Rights Act in respect to terrorist offences. This would have been virtually impossible in the US in the same timescale.

Critics also warn of the danger of handing more political power to the judiciary. A US-style Supreme Court could see unaccountable judges straying into the political arena. Indeed, many recent senior judicial appointments in the USA point to this being a concern of some presidents. It could be argued, too, that this would lead to a further loss of political accountability, in that a codified constitution would see less power being wielded by elected politicians and more political judgements being made in courts.

A codified constitution may also lead to weak government. In the United States, for example, the president and Congress (who may be from different political parties) can find themselves in conflict over issues, leading to inaction. In the mid-1990s, President Clinton, the Democratic president of the US, was at loggerheads with the House of Representatives, in which the Republicans held a majority. Their inability to agree led to an acute federal budget crisis, causing political gridlock in Washington.

Furthermore, one could argue that, far from enhancing political accountability, a codified constitution is more likely to bring a blurring of accountability, and again the United States provides an insight into this. In the above-mentioned stalemate between President Clinton and the House of Representatives in 1995, it was difficult for many people to apportion blame accurately. Although President Clinton appeared to win in terms of popular opinion, many on the Republican side believed that an injustice was done. This contrasts with the UK's uncodified system, where there is clear accountability for the UK government. Since it is able to carry out its programme, the people can apportion credit or blame accordingly. A government may try, but usually without success, to blame other institutions for its own omissions or mistakes.

🗩 The first point is relevant because the issue of separate lines of accountability is directly related to the relative unchangeability of a codified constitution. It is important that points are made relevant to the question by proper explanation and the use of appropriate examples.

The two subsequent points deal with important advantages of a codified constitution. Both are well explained and illustrated with relevant examples. In the case of the point about amending a codified constitution, there is a direct reference to the UK system. The final sentence of the paragraph makes this example relevant to the response.

The argument in defence of a codified constitution is well made and emphasised by references to both the US and the UK. It is important to stress the strength of something, but it also helps if these strengths can be contrasted with the weaknesses of alternatives.

The arguments against a codified constitution also deploy useful material from the United States example as well as good descriptions of the points made.

This response is about 1,000 words long and would require a writing rate of about 25 words per minute if all 40 minutes were utilised in answering the question. It contains a number of points that have been well explained and illustrated with relevant examples. In addition, both of the sides of the debate have been covered in the answer. This essay would score about 35 marks out of the total of 40 marks available.

■ ■ ■

C-grade answer

Codified constitutions set out the powers enjoyed by different political institutions in a country. In the United States, for example, the president's role is set out in the Constitution. The people know how the power of the state is divided up between the legislature and the executive, for example.

A second point in favour of codified constitutions is that they curb the power of the government. The UK government has the power do almost whatever it likes and can only be constrained by Parliament. Governments usually have majorities in Parliament and this enables them to govern without any real check on power. In the US, the codified Constitution limits the power of the government and restricts the range of things that the government can do.

A codified constitution is difficult to change, which once again restricts the powers of the government. In the United States, changes to the Constitution need to clear hurdles in both the US Congress and the 50 states. Without such agreement there can be no amendment of the Constitution. In the UK system, governments can effectively change the constitution by making a law, for example extending the life of Parliament. It can be seen therefore that countries with codified constitutions remain freer from political interference than those that have uncodified constitutions.

Opponents warn that there would be significant risks in the UK of adopting a codified constitution. Codified constitutions give too much power to judges. Judges are not elected and so it could be argued that this would be less democratic.

Britain would be losing a tried and tested model. The UK constitution has evolved over centuries and is best fitted to the country. Many of the central aspects of the political order (parliamentary sovereignty, for example) would be lost if the system were reformed in such a way.

🖉 The initial point is a valid one, but the implications of this first paragraph are not made sufficiently explicit. The key argument that should have been developed was the issue of accountability. There is no mention of the idea that because a codified constitution specifies which body or person is responsible for a particular function or responsibility, they can be more easily held accountable for their actions. It is quite possible that this point was intended, but if it is not clearly stated, the examiner cannot 'dig' beneath the words looking for added meaning.

The second part of the answer gives a fairly accurate description of the strength of a codified constitution in relation to the power of the executive. There are accurate references to both the US and the UK, but no examples are given to illustrate the point made.

The next point is essentially correct in that it points to the relative difficulty in amending a codified constitution. This part of the response, however, does not say much else. If anything, the response is a little dogmatic in that it makes assumptions about all codified constitutions. It should be stressed that a codified constitution is only difficult to amend if that is what is specified in the constitution. Perhaps 'Codified constitutions are *usually* more difficult to change...' would have been a better way to begin.

The example given for this point is hypothetical — something that could happen. It would have been better to have used a real example.

The main problem with this response, however, is that it is unbalanced. There are a couple of points made on each side of the debate, but the arguments against a codified constitution are sketchier. There is little or no development of the arguments and not much illustrative material.

Overall this response is thinner than the A-grade answer. It covers less ground and misses out any discussion of the protection of the rights of the citizen. Those points that are made are given an inadequate level of explanation and are in no sense full answers. Finally, there is a shortage of good examples which would show an ability to apply the knowledge demonstrated in the rest of the answer. This response would earn 17 or 18 marks.

Question 4

The judiciary and civil liberties

To what extent are judges in the UK independent and neutral?

Like Question 3, this is an essay question. It carries 40 marks and candidates have about 40 minutes in which to answer it. However, unlike Question 3, two distinct political concepts are being assessed. There are therefore four parts to be covered in this question: examining the case for and against judicial independence, and for and against judicial neutrality. Although marks are not awarded in blocks of 10, this gives you some idea of the number of marks you could miss out on for only partial coverage of this question.

■ ■ ■

A-grade answer

Judicial independence refers to the notion that judges remain separate from the other parts of the UK political system. In the first instance, judges have security of tenure. This means that they cannot easily be dismissed. Because of this, judges do not have to worry about their jobs while doing their work. Furthermore, judges' pay is not decided upon by politicians but by an independent salary review body. All this means that judges are free from any personal pressures that might interfere with decisions they make. When the then Lord Chief Justice, Lord Woolf, criticised the government's sentencing policy in July 2004, he did so knowing that he would not be sacked as a consequence.

Recent reforms to the way judges are appointed means that ministers have less influence over the formation of the judiciary. Vacancies are now advertised and interviews for judicial positions are conducted by an independent appointment panel.

Third, judges are legally immune from civil actions arising as a consequence of their capacity as judges. This means that during the course of a trial, judges are protected by the law over the events that go on there. If this were not so, the judge would not feel free to conduct a court case in the way he or she felt fit and this could impair the process of justice.

Finally, there is a parliamentary convention that judges are not criticised in Parliament. This is important, as it protects judges from undue political interference. The convention also protects politicians from being drawn into judicial territory by the media or pressure groups. During the controversy about Lord Hoffman being one of the House of Lords judges to decide on the extradition of General Pinochet, Members of Parliament were restrained in their comments about this matter.

There are a number of concerns about the extent to which judges are truly independent of the other agents of the UK constitution. Senior members of the judiciary are still appointed by the executive. It may be argued that there is potential for political interference in the careers of senior judges and that this calls into question the extent to which judges are politically independent. At present the appointment process is carried out in secrecy. There is an informal selection system, based on the 'sounding out' of individuals for judicial appointment.

The Law Lords remain members the House of Lords. This overlap of powers makes it difficult to argue that there is true independence for members of the judiciary, not only because of the impact that their proximity to the political system might have on them, but also because of the impact that they, as unelected individuals, might have upon the democratic system.

Although the judiciary is theoretically free from political interference, they are subject to media interest and pressure. While it is proper that the media ensure public opinion is taken into account by judges, it is a worry that this may be going too far. There have been a number of high-profile cases where the press has criticised sentences given out by judges, and pressure has been put on the government to act. Many newspapers criticised the sentence given to Maxine Carr for her part in the Soham murder case. The home secretary, Michael Howard, felt compelled to interfere with the sentences given to the killers of James Bulger.

The theory of judicial neutrality states that, regardless of their social background, personal beliefs or political leanings, judges must act in a way that does not exhibit bias. In a court case, a judge must not allow any of these matters to sway the way that he or she conducts a trial. Similarly, when judges are dealing with a matter for judicial review, they should not be influenced by anything other than the facts and the law.

Judicial neutrality is founded upon the fundamental principle that justice ought to be blind to all factors that are not of relevance to the matter before the court or the judge in chambers. In this way, everyone should be equal in the eyes of the courts and it is the duty of the judge to apply such equality. This theory is an essential foundation of the law in that otherwise there could be no consistency in the application of law.

Judicial neutrality has been criticised by Griffiths, who argued that judges were in the main Oxbridge-educated, white, male (95% of judges are men), and upper-middle class with conservative tendencies. Some say this view has been demonstrated in a number of court cases. During the Ponting trial, where a civil servant claimed he acted in the national interest when he leaked secrets about the sinking of an Argentine cruiser during the Falklands War in 1982, the judge advised the jury that it was for the government to decide what was in the national interest.

During the 1984–85 miners' strike, judges appeared to side with the government and employers against the National Union of Mineworkers when matters reached the courts. Some saw this as anti-union bias by members of the judiciary, and a clear endorsement of what Griffiths had said of them.

Earlier in the 1980s the Labour-led Greater London Council's policy of cheap public transport fares was challenged in the courts. The Master of the Rolls, Lord Denning, ruled against the GLC, which was then forced to abandon the policy. Once again, some on the left saw this as a decision arising from the clear bias and personal beliefs of Denning himself.

In defence of the theory of judicial neutrality, there is large body of cases and decisions where the impartiality of the judiciary cannot be challenged because they have been based upon the evidence and the law. Indeed, judges have been willing to rule against Conservative governments as well as Labour. In 1985, the government was defeated by the courts on social security reforms. There were also cases where judges found against Conservative home secretary Kenneth Baker.

In the early 1990s the courts halted the government's pit closure programme after an appeal by the National Union of Mineworkers, pending a proper review. Around the same time a judge threw out a case prosecuting the directors of the Matrix Churchill company, because he believed that ministerial actions were denying the defendants natural justice.

🖉 This response copes with the demands of the question very well in a number of respects. In the first instance, there is an attempt to state what both the theories of judicial independence and judicial neutrality mean. This is then tested in both theoretical and practical terms. The answer gives a balanced analysis, offering both sides of the debate for each concept. It is well explained and includes a number of useful and relevant examples

This response would receive an A grade because of the level of understanding it shows, the extent to which there is real evaluation, the use of appropriate examples and a strong conclusion. It would earn 34–36 marks.

■ ■ ■

C-grade answer

Judges are independent because they are protected from government interference. Their salaries are not set by government ministers. They cannot easily be sacked and they are rarely criticised by politicians. This means that judges are able to get on with their jobs without having to look over their shoulders for ministerial intervention.

Judges are recruited through the legal system from the pool of barristers, and unlike the judiciary in a number of countries, are not formally trained to be judges by the government. Again, this maintains a distance between politicians and members of the judiciary.

Judges are not neutral because they have shown bias to the Conservatives over the years. It is clear that most judges are white, old and middle class, having studied at Oxford and Cambridge universities. This background makes it difficult for them to see life from the point of view of ordinary people, and this is why many of the decisions they take cannot be seen as neutral.

Over the past 50 years there have been a number of cases where judges have not appeared to be neutral. During the trial of Clive Ponting, a Ministry of Defence civil servant who leaked government papers about the sinking of the Argentine battleship, *Belgrano*, Ponting's defence was that he was acting in the national interest. The judge in the case was accused of bias when he advised the jury that it was the government that determined what was and was not in the national interest, and not an individual civil servant.

In the 1980s, the Thatcher government attempted to halt the publication of *Spycatcher*, the memoirs of Peter Wright, who used to work for MI5. Judges upheld the government's objection to the publication of the book and it was banned for some time. Again, this shows how willing judges were to side with Conservative governments against individuals who seemed to be challenging the political establishment.

This response does not fully answer the question; candidates were being invited to evaluate the concepts of judicial independence and neutrality, which requires two sides of the debate to be put across for each concept. Unlike the A-grade answer, this response does not attempt to present a balance of opinion.

Both concepts are covered, but only partially. The first part of the answer deals with judicial independence, but only explains what it is without any evaluation. There is no real explanation of judicial neutrality, but rather a general theoretical critique of the concept and two substantial examples. The scope of the response is limited to examples from the 1980s with no attempt to draw upon recent developments, which would show that the candidate had an up-to-date understanding of judicial neutrality. This answer would gain **17–18 marks**.